"Carol's skills as a teache well-written books and speaki... with and is always well-prepared and well-versed in her subjects. I highly recommend her." —Sharon Siepel, author of *Essential Survival Guide to Living on Your Own*

"I read Carol Topp's book, *Business Tips and Taxes for Writers* and kept thinking, "Now I understand! Why didn't someone explain it that way before?" Carol has a knack for making confusing topics clear and putting complex subjects such as taxes and inventory in a nutshell. Her book is an easy but essential, read." —Mary Hood, Ph.D., author of *The Relaxed Home School*

"A must read for authors! Carol Topp makes these difficult concepts easy to understand. *Business Tips and Taxes for Writers* is full of helpful information encouraging writers to be able to run a profitable business." —JoJo Tabares, Author, Publisher at Art of Eloquence

"Carol Topp's *Business Tips and Taxes for Writers* is essential for setting up your business, minimizing your mistakes, and maximizing your profits!" —Cathy Diez-Luckie, publisher at FiguresInMotion.com

"This book is THE book I have been looking for since I began writing. This is a handy reference for those who are ready to take their writing seriously and get busy building a successful business. Every page is packed full of applicable information—TODAY! This information is so needed by busy writers of blogs, articles, or books. Everything you could ever need to know is covered—from setting up your business, learning how to claim your expenses and profits, what's required and how to make record keeping a breeze—it is all covered in this dynamic book. This quick read will save you money immediately. And, believe me, you'll be referencing this book often. Just like a personal CPA all along the way." —Cindy Rushton, writer, speaker, business coach, and radio show host. TheBizMentor.com

Information in a Nutshell™
BUSINESS TIPS AND TAXES FOR WRITERS

BY

CAROL TOPP, CPA

Media Angels,® Inc.
Fort Myers, Florida

Information in a Nutshell™: Business Tips and Taxes for Writers
© 2012, 2016 by Carol Topp, CPA

Published by Media Angels, ® Inc.
Fort Myers, FL 33912
www.MediaAngels.com

ISBN: 978-1-931941-33-4
ISBN: Electronic Edition: 978-1-931941-22-8

Original Cover Design: Jessica Dowling Hammer
Layout: Edward Cook
Editor: Viktorija Girton

Printed in the United States of America

CONTENTS

For many writers, the freelance life is a dream come true. We can work from anywhere in the world, write about subjects we find fascinating, and fit our working hours around our family and personal needs. It *is* a dream life—as long as we can ignore the number monster that lurks at the fringe of consciousness.

The number monster demands that we track expenses, fill out tax forms, and create cash flow projections. For those of us who escaped as many math classes as possible, these tasks are not only stressful and often confusing, but they also take time from doing the things we love (and the things that pay the bills).

Even though most of us manage the basics, there's always a nagging feeling that we may be missing something, or just plain doing it wrong. Visions of an IRS audit haunt our dreams. And just when we think the number monster has been vanquished, another month rolls around and there it is again. And don't even mention tax time . . .

Sir Francis Bacon tells us that knowledge is power and I'm here to tell you that it's a comfort as well. Carol Topp's concise book takes a writer-friendly look at the financial information freelancers need in order to tame the number monster. She walks us through financial planning, business structure, a simple bookkeeping system, inventory, taxes, working with an accountant, and more, finishing with interviews with the owners of several writing-based businesses. Best of all, the entire book is written in plain, kitchen-table English.

As an entrepreneurial writer and business owner, I've had to face the number monster more times than I care to remember. If I'd had Carol's book when I started, the journey it would have been much less daunting and I might not have made so many of the common mistakes she describes. No matter where you are in your writing journey, this little book will be a comforting and helpful companion.

Janice Campbell
Director, National Association of Independent Writers and Editors

INTRODUCTION

Writers know that words matter. A correctly placed word has the ability to convey meaning and nuance. Each profession had its unique jargon and the world of business and taxes is no exception. Unfortunately, business language can confuse many writers. This book clarifies difficult topics and makes them clear and understandable in a concise way—it offers information in a nutshell.

I know that many authors hate dealing with numbers—especially with dollar signs or on a tax form. When I discuss a complex business issue such as inventory, I share examples drawn for real life. I tell you what you need to know and what you can entrust to your CPA.

As an author and accountant, I strive to be an interpreter between the confusing language of business and you, the writer, author or publisher. I understand both the vocabulary of the IRS and the mind of a writer. I do not want your writing business to fail or even flounder for lack of information. I have seen many authors struggle financially because they lacked the proper understanding of the business world or, in more than one case, a tax form..

While this book is not an exhaustive resource of everything you need to know about starting or running a small business, it focuses on the most important issues for a writer. Here you will find a discussion on your choice of business structure: hobby, ministry, sole proprietorship, partnership or corporation. The pros and cons of each option are explored, allowing you to make an informed decision.

Chapters include tips on start up expenses, organizing your records and using software, which will help you stay organized as your writing or publishing business grows. I will show you a simple way to record your expenses, so you can focus your time on writing, not bookkeeping. A chapter on inventory gives vital information if you purchase your own books and resell them to readers. Then, I discuss sales tax from an author's perspective and briefly go over a business tax return for a sole proprietorship, highlighting the important parts that confuse many authors. After reading those chapters, you should feel as if you have just met with your CPA and learned important information.

Finally, the book offers tips on mistakes to avoid, a chapter with writers discussing their businesses, and a resource list of books and websites. These resources will help you run your business smoothly, allowing you to focus on what you do best—writing.

Carol Topp, CPA

CHAPTER 1

WRITING AS A HOBBY

Many authors start writing as a hobby and do it for the love of writing. They may have a blog or occasionally submit an article to a magazine, but making money is not a strong motivator—writing for pleasure compels them. Occasionally, a hobby author may receive payment for her work. Does this automatically make her a professional author? Perhaps not, but the income must still be reported as earned income on the tax return. The Internal Revenue Service (IRS) has guidelines to help hobbyists know where and how to report income.

Hobby or Business?

How do you know if you have a hobby or a business? There is no set dollar threshold that changes a hobby writer into a professional. It depends primarily on your motivation for writing. The IRS has a few factors to consider:

- The time and effort you spend in the activity can determine hobby status. Spending significant amounts of time writing might imply that your writing is more than a hobby and it is a business.
- The manner you conduct the activity such as doing advertising or bookkeeping may mean your hobby has become a business.
- Your expertise and prior success in a similar activity may cause your hobby to be classified as a business. An author with a publishing contract has a business, not a hobby.
- Your profit motive and prior history of profits may indicate a for-profit business, not a hobby.
- Other sources of income may demonstrate your writing is not your main source of income, but only a hobby.[1]

The IRS has an article titled *Is Your Hobby a For-Profit Endeavor?* that you can find at www.irs.gov/ by searching on "hobby income."

Hobby Income

Income, even from a hobby, has to be reported to the IRS. Hobby income is usually reported on the individual tax return (Form 1040) under Other Income (Line 21 on the 2010 Form 1040).

Example: Mary wrote several magazine articles as a hobby but had never been paid. Finally, a magazine published an article and paid Mary $250. She is thrilled and called her tax preparer to discuss how to report this income. Mary will probably not receive any tax documentation from the magazine for the $250 payment. Payments to independent contractors over $600 a year must be reported to the worker on Form 1099MISC. Since Mary received only $250, she will not receive a 1099MISC from the magazine. It is still her responsibility to report this income even if she does not receive any other paperwork from the magazine.

1 Source: www.irs.gov/businesses/small/article/0,,id=208400,00.html#appendix01

Hobby Expenses

Expenses can be deducted on Form 1040 Schedule A Itemized Deductions under Miscellaneous Deductions, subject to a 2% of adjusted gross income threshold. This threshold means that a taxpayer can deduct miscellaneous deductions that are *greater* than 2% of their adjusted gross income.

Example: Mary's tax preparer puts Mary's income of $250 on the Form 1040 under Other Income. Mary's only expenses related to this income are paper, ink and postage. Mary's expenses can be deducted on her itemized deductions under miscellaneous deductions, subject to 2% of her adjusted gross income. As is common with many taxpayers, Mary's miscellaneous deductions were too small to overcome the 2% threshold to be deductible. She received no tax deduction for her writing expenses.

Some hobby writers pay the printing costs of their books. This is considered a cost of selling, or in accounting jargon, the cost of goods sold. The IRS allows a taxpayer to deduct the cost of goods sold from their hobby income. Only the net amount of income is reported as other income.

Example, Tom, a hobby writer, wrote his life story in a book and had 50 copies printed to sell to friends at $10 each. The printing costs were $150. Tom received total income of $500 from sales of his book. He reports hobby income of only $350 ($500 sales—$150 printing costs). Any other writing expenses unrelated to the book production costs are deducted as miscellaneous deductions on Schedule A, subject to 2% of Tom's adjusted gross income.

No Hobby Losses Allowed

For tax purposes, the IRS does not allow hobby expenses to exceed hobby income. In other words, losses from a hobby are not permitted on a tax return. A business can have a loss and it can be deducted on a tax return, but not a hobby loss. If John, a hobby writer, attended a writers workshop and his expenses of $900 exceeded his hobby income of $400, he could deduct his expenses (as miscellaneous deductions) up to the amount of his income, but no more. The extra expenses of $500 are considered personal expenses that John incurred for the love of writing.

In a Nutshell:

The advantage of considering your writing as a hobby is that you avoid the complications of filing a business tax return. The major disadvantage to hobby writing is that your expenses may not be a tax deduction and hobby losses are not deductible. Overall, a hobby writer rarely expects or is eligible for any tax benefits. If your writing hobby is producing regular income, it is time to consider it a business. Chapter Three discusses writing as a business.

CHAPTER 2

WRITING AS A MINISTRY

In the previous chapter, I discussed writing as a hobby done for pleasure and without a profit motive. A writing hobby may grow to become a more serious venture and generate money, but it can still lack a profit motive. In these cases, the author may believe her writing is a gift to her readers and sometimes sees her business as a ministry. A writer may receive payment for selling a book or articles, but her passion is the message, not making a profit. It is common for every penny earned to go back into the business to purchase supplies and pay expenses such as traveling and printing. The business is run without a profit motive, but could it be a classified as a for-profit business for tax purposes? An author might wonder, "What is the tax status for a business that is really more of a ministry?"

The Internal Revenue Service (IRS) does not have a category called "ministry" for tax purposes, but they do have two other categories: charitable nonprofits and for-profit businesses. A writing ministry can be structured as either.

Charitable Nonprofit Organization

A charitable nonprofit organization is an entity that has a mission other than making money. The mission can be to promote education, further religion, provide relief of the poor, eliminate prejudice, defend human rights or combat juvenile delinquency (these are just examples, not an exhaustive list). Charitable nonprofits can be quite large such as the Red Cross or small such as a local church.

The distinction between nonprofit and for-profit businesses are:
- Profit motive. A charitable organization is motivated by its mission, not profit. A for-profit business is primarily motivated to earn a profit for its owner(s).
- Ownership. No one owns a charity. A board of directors and staff run the organization, but they are not owners in the same sense that a sole proprietor, partnership or shareholders own a for-profit business.
- Use of surplus money. A charity may accumulate a surplus, but it does not belong to the board or the staff. Surplus money stays in the charitable organization for use in the future toward its purpose. The word nonprofit is slightly misleading because charitable organizations can make a profit; it just does not distribute the profit to any owner. For-profits distribute profits to the owners, partners or shareholders every year.

Example: Cheryl Cook of Heavenly C. Ministries (www. HeavenlyCMin.org), writes about the Christian family. She is passionate about her topic and considers her writing a ministry. For several years Cheryl sold books and filed a tax return as a sole proprietorship, sometimes showing a small profit and sometimes showing a loss. She and her husband felt led to expand their ministry, conduct workshops and travel to conventions. They would like to solicit donations to offset their travel expenses. They gathered advisers, established a board members and obtained "qualified charity" status with the IRS as a 501(c)(3) educational organization.

IRS Qualified Charity

In Cheryl's story above, I mention 501(c)(3) organizations. These are charitable nonprofit organizations that are granted a special tax status by the IRS. Most charitable nonprofits seek 501(c)(3) status from the IRS for the tax advantages and the ability to receive tax-deductible donations. The official definition of 501(c)(3) organizations from the IRS website is:

"...organized and operated exclusively for religious, charitable, scientific, testing for public safety, literary, or educational purposes, or to foster national or international amateur sports competition, or for the prevention of cruelty to children or animals."

There are other types of nonprofit organizations such as social clubs and professional organizations. They are considered tax exempt by the IRS and are classified as 501(c)(4) and 501(c)(7) organizations. There are 13 different types of 501c organizations, but only 501(c)(3)'s may accept tax deductible donations. 501(c)(3) organizations are by far the most popular type, with more than 80% of tax exempt organizations being classified as 501(c)(3)s.

Running a Business as a Ministry

An author with a mission in mind could run a ministry as a for-profit venture. Naturally, if the author spends all she earns there is no profit and therefore no income tax to pay. The tax return will look much like a small business tax return, but with very little or no profit. There may even be a loss in some years. If a loss is recorded too many years in a row (typically three out of five years), the IRS may determine the business is a hobby and not allow losses greater than income. If you find yourself in a situation where your expenses from your writing ministry exceeds your income (i.e. you have a loss) for several years in a row, consult a Certified Public Accountant (CPA).

He or she can be a great help in determining the correct business structure. You may consider qualified charity status with the IRS or restructure your for-profit business to come closer to breaking even or even make a profit.

Example: JoJo Tabares has run an organization called The Art of Eloquence for several years. She calls it her ministry because she devotes a lot of time toward teaching communication skills. She is passionate about her topic and gives away a lot of information via her website, articles, podcasts and seminars. She funds her "ministry" by selling books and ebooks. JoJo is the sole owner of her enterprise and hopes to make a small profit each year. Any profit she makes is hers to spend as she wishes and she usually uses the surplus to build her business. In terms of her business structure, JoJo operates a for-profit business.

Can an Author Start a 501(c)(3) Charitable Organization?

A sole individual or a family cannot establish an IRS qualified charity by themselves; a charity must be governed by a board of leaders. Alternatively, a publishing company can apply for 501 (c) (3) tax exempt status and indeed several publishing companies have obtained the coveted status from the IRS.

Here is the mission statement of a 501(c)(3) organization that publishes the books of author Mary Hood and its mission statement:

ARCHERS for the Lord ® is a non-profit 501c(3) organization that grew out of the ideas of its founder, Mary Hood, nationally known as "The Relaxed Home Schooler®". She is the author of such books as *The Relaxed Home School, The Joyful Home Schooler* and *Countdown to Consistency.*

She believes that a "relaxed home school" develops out of the mindset that you are a family, not a school; a dad, not a principal; a mom, not a teacher; and that you have individual relationships with your children, not a classroom. This mindset helps you to stress out less over school-like expectations, and relax and enjoy your family. (Source www.archersforthelord.org)

As you can see from their mission statement, ARCHERS for the Lord® has a specific purpose. Writing and publishing are a means to accomplish that purpose.

Advantages of Qualified Charity Status for Publishers

Although an individual cannot be a 501(c)(3) charity, an organization can be granted the status. It may not be common for a single author to be granted 501(c)(3) status, but a publishing company might find the status has many benefits.

Tax exemption

The IRS grants tax exempt status to nonprofit organizations that qualify. Tax exemption means that the profit a charity makes from its charitable purpose is tax free and can be used to further the mission of the organization.

Contributions

Contributions of cash or property to a qualified charity are tax-deductible. The qualified charity status usually boosts donations to an organization significantly. Many grants and foundations will only give funds to qualified 501(c)(3) organizations.

Discounts and Special programs

There are other benefits of 501(c)(3) status including special discounts on postage and discounts on rent or equipment offered by some businesses. Some states offer special status to nonprofits such as sales-tax exemptions on purchases made by the nonprofit or property tax exemptions. Additionally, some communities have discounted office supply stores only open to 501(c)(3) organizations and large companies give away software and computers to 501(c)(3) organizations.

Disadvantages of 501(c)(3) Status

Before you launch into the application for 501(c)(3) tax exempt status, you should know some of the disadvantages including time, money, political limitations and required reporting to the IRS.

Cost

Obtaining IRS tax exempt status is a difficult and time consuming process, especially for an author that simply wishes to write as a ministry. The costs to apply for 501(c)(3) tax exempt status can add up. The application fee to the IRS is $400 for organizations with gross annual revenues under $10,000. The fee increases to $850 for organizations with gross annual revenues over $10,000. As of this writing, the IRS has plans to lower the application fee to $200 for all organizations that apply using a new on-line system, called Cyber Assistant, set to launch in 2011 or later.

Many organizations hire professional assistance from either a lawyer or an accountant to help them with the IRS application (Form 1023). I offer my services to nonprofit organizations desiring to apply for 501(c)(3) status or to file their annual IRS report, Form 990. You can read more about my services to nonprofits at CarolToppCPA.com

Paperwork

The paperwork to apply for 501(c)(3) status can be daunting. The application form for the IRS (Form 1023) is 28 pages long. The instructions for Form 1023 are another 38 pages long. The actual package you mail to the IRS could be 30-50 pages due to the IRS requirement for these documents:

❑ Bylaws
❑ Articles of Incorporation or "organizing documents"
❑ Policy manuals
❑ Mission or purpose statements

- ❏ Explanation of activities
- ❏ History of your organization
- ❏ List of Board Members names and addresses
- ❏ Five years of financial statements
- ❏ List of donors and amounts donated

Political Limitations and Required Reporting

In addition to cost and paperwork, the IRS imposes other limitations on 501(c)(3) organizations. Qualified charities are limited in their political activities. The IRS never intended for 501(c)(3) organizations to collect tax deductible donations that could then be funneled to a political candidate. For that reason, 501(c)(3) organizations are limited in their political activities. A 501(c)(3) organization can lobby for legislation, but cannot endorse a candidate for local, state or federal office. Nonpartisan educational activities are allowed.

The IRS also imposes annual reporting from qualified charities. Most 501(c)(3) organizations must file an annual information return called Form 990 with the IRS. The Form 990 has questions about activities, finances, fund raising, donations and board members. Organizations with annual revenues under $50,000 file a short on-line version called a 990N.

Ownership

No one owns a charity. The board of directors control the organization. The founder of a nonprofit does not fully own or control the organization. Unfortunately a founder can be voted off the board by the other directors. Be aware that in starting a nonprofit organization, you will give up control of the organization to a board of directors even if you handpicked these individuals.

Example: Two women desired to offer education programs to children and wished to receive donations and grants to run the programs. They consulted me about forming a 501(c)(3) organization. I explained that they would not "own" the organization, but would have to relinquish control of the group to the board of directors. The founders planned to be on the board, but they understood that they could be voted off at any time. They wisely reconsidered their decision and formed a for-profit business, so that they could retain control of the program.

Consider carefully the pros and cons of obtaining 501(c)(3) tax exempt status as a charity. Start by reading the IRS website for charities www.irs.gov/eo and discussing the option with several advisers including a qualified attorney and a CPA.

Process to Obtain Qualified Charity Status

In order to be classified as a qualified charity by the Internal Revenue Service, your organization must have a charitable purpose, lack a profit motive, be run by a board of directors and adopt bylaws. It is usually recommended that charities also establish themselves as nonprofit corporations in their state. Here's a check list to see if your organization is ready:

- Do you have a mission statement?
- Do you have a board of directors, regular meetings and a method to elect the board?
- Do you have bylaws and articles of incorporation or a charter, usually called the organization's governing documents?
- Do you keep minutes of your meetings?
- Do you have five years of financial history or if your organization is new, can you estimate two years of future financial statements?
- Would you be willing to forgo any political candidate endorsements? 501(c)(3) organizations may not endorse political candidates, but they can lobby for legislation.

- Do you have enough money to pay the IRS filing fee of $200-$850?

On my website, www.CarolToppCPA.com, I have a checklist of tasks to complete when filing for 501(c)(3) status. If you are considering pursuing 501(c)(3) status for your publishing company, you may find this information extremely useful.

501(c)(3) Status for Publishing Companies and the IRS

If you are a publishing company (or considering becoming a publisher), the IRS has some helpful information. In a report titled, *501(c)(3) Organizations and Publishing Activities,* the IRS gives guidance on the difference between exempt publishing activities and commercial publishing activities. This report is a training guide for IRS employees and may not be light reading for most authors. Nevertheless, you should be aware that the IRS has published guidance that your attorney or CPA will find helpful if you intend to file for tax exempt 501(c)(3) status. Share this report with your attorney or CPA You can find it at http://IRS.gov and search for "501c3 Publishing Activities." Chapter 17 Resources has the complete link.

In a Nutshell

Writing as a ministry is a noble pursuit. Some authors run their ministries as a for-profit business and barely make a profit. Other writers form nonprofit organizations and seek the benefits of qualified charity 501(c)(3) status with the IRS. Although an individual author cannot be a qualified charity, a publishing company may consider the status. In the next four chapters, I will cover for-profit business structures including sole proprietorships, partnerships, corporations and limited liability companies.

CHAPTER THREE

SOLE PROPRIETORSHIP

Many writers begin as hobbyists. Eventually, a hobby may grow to the point that it becomes a serious, profit-focused venture. Perhaps one of your goals is to be profitable. Each person's needs varies and your writing can help produce income to meet those needs. Wouldn't that be wonderful? But running your writing as a business requires some special knowledge and the acquisition of new skills. Among those necessary skills are record keeping, taxes, and other business matters. The remainder of this book contains valuable information to give you many of the tools you need to make informative business tax decisions.

The best place to start in forming a writing business is to carefully consider your business structure. There are several different business structures. The most common business structure for authors is the sole proprietorship. However, some authors form partnerships or corporations. Following is a discussion of these options so you can determine which structure is best for you.

Characteristics of a Sole Proprietorship

The vast majority of authors are sole proprietorships with good reason. It is the simplest business structure—easy to start and easy to close. A sole proprietorship is a business with one owner. It is popular with writers for many reasons:

- Quick to start. You are in business as soon as you say that you are or at least when you are paid for your writing. I went from a hobby writer to a "professional" when I received $50 for a magazine article. A business was born the day I received the check.

- Minimal filings. Usually a writer can use her own name as the business name, so no DBA (Doing Business As) name filing is needed. A publishing company might use a fictitious name and should register their name with their state. The rules vary by state and county. Do an internet search on your state name and "business registration" or "secretary of state." It should lead to the regulations and proper forms for your state. When in doubt, call your secretary of state; the phone number is on their website.

- Easy to close. Partnerships and corporations are sometimes more work to shut down than to start up, but a sole proprietorship closes down when the owner makes this decision.

- Easy to understand. Partnerships and corporations can be very complex and difficult to understand. On the other hand, you probably know someone who operates a small business as a sole proprietorship and can understand what they do.

- Simplest tax structure. A sole proprietorship has a fairly simple tax structure compared to partnerships and corporations. Sole proprietors use a two page form (Schedule C Business Income or Loss) and attach it to their personal tax return.

Partnerships and corporations require completely separate multi-page tax returns *and* additional forms that are added to the owners' individual tax returns.

- No lawyer needed to start. Many sole proprietorships form their own business without the assistance of a lawyer. I do recommend you hire an attorney to look over any publishing contracts before you sign. I hired a lawyer to review the contract for this book. I did not need her legal services to start my sole proprietorship. I strongly recommend hiring an attorney if you are forming a partnership or corporation because of their complexity.

- Simplified record keeping. Like any business, a sole proprietorship needs to keep good records, but it can be simple. Many sole proprietors can do their own bookkeeping. They typically hire an accountant for an initial consultant and for tax preparation.

- You keep the profits. Partnerships and corporations distribute their profits to partners or shareholders, but a sole proprietorship owns all the profit (after taxes, of course!).

- No investors to keep happy. You, the owner, need to be happy with your business progress, not outside investors or partners.

Chapter Eight is devoted to record keeping, but here are some tips for sole proprietors on important documents in the start up of a new business.

Tax ID Number

Many writers start their business and give their Social Security number (SSN) when expecting payment from publishers who require this information. Since identity theft is pervasive, I recommend you consider obtaining an Employer Identification Number (EIN) from the Internal Revenue Service to keep your Social Security number private. An EIN is like a Social Security number for businesses. You can receive the number from the IRS on-line in minutes for no charge. Go to www.IRS.gov and type "EIN" in the search box.

Example: Ann was to receive a form 1099MISC for income she had been paid during the year, and the payer had requested her Social Security number. Since she had an EIN, I encouraged her to give the payer her EIN and keep her Social Security number private to avoid identity theft. Either an SSN or EIN may be used on the Form 1099MISC, although the IRS prefers that sole proprietors use their SSN.

Business Name

Usually, you can use your own name as your business name and do not need to file a fictitious name registration, called a DBA (Doing Business As) name filing, with your state or county. If you form a publishing company you will probably choose a business name. Check with your Secretary of State to see if the name is available and to determine their name registration requirements. Search www.business.gov and use the keywords "fictitious business name" for requirements for filing a fictitious business name in each state.

Example: For many years, I ran my accounting practice using only my name, Carol Topp, CPA. It was easy. That name was on my business cards and checking account. No fictitious name or DBA registration was needed. Then I created a publishing company, Ambassador Publishing, and started doing business under its name. I then registered that DBA name with Ohio's Secretary of State, filling out a one page document with a $50 fee.

Business Checking Account

Business owners are usually advised to open a separate checking account for their business. Sometimes sole proprietorships fear a separate account will be expensive or cumbersome, but it is not so. Many banks offer free checking to small businesses. A separate business account is not more work; it can actually simplify record keeping because you will avoid mixing personal and business expenses. Separating business and personal expenses in a mixed account is a waste of precious time and you might have to pay your tax preparer to do it for you. It is much easier to have separate accounts.

Example: I was categorizing Mike's transactions from his business checking account to prepare his tax return and noticed debit card charges at the grocery store, several restaurants and the doctor's office. These were clearly personal expenses and not business related. Mike had committed a serious offense (in the eyes of his tax preparer!) and he had to pay for my time to sort it all out. Instead, Mike should have used his personal account for his family expenses and saved his business checking account solely for business related expenses.

In a Nutshell

A sole proprietorship is an easy and swift way to start a writing or publishing business. In an upcoming chapter, I profile several authors who started as sole proprietorships and remained that way because it suited their needs. Alternatively, authors may chose different business structures such as partnerships or corporations. The next three chapters cover these options.

CHAPTER FOUR

PARTNERSHIPS

Occasionally, a writer may co-author a book or establish a business relationship with another person. Sometimes these agreements are informal working arrangements or mutually beneficial projects. These agreements may be a working partnership, but are not a formal business structure. There is a big difference. To the IRS and accountants, partnerships are a formal business structure with more than one owner.

Example: I meet with Brent, a new small business owner who told me he was a sole proprietor. I got very confused when he mentioned a partner. "I thought you were a sole proprietor," I asked. "Oh, yeah, well I have this guy who did my website that never charged me. I thought I'd make him a partner and split the profits." Bad idea. I discussed the pros and cons of having a partner. Instead, I encouraged him to pay the web designer over time and avoid a complicated partnership agreement.

Taxes for Partnerships

Partnerships are not taxed as a separate entity, but rather are "pass through" businesses, meaning that any profit or loss is passed to the partners and reported on their tax returns. The tax preparation and record keeping for partnerships can become quite complicated because each partners' contribution to the business must be recorded. I highly recommend you hire a competent Certified Public Accountant (CPA) to prepare your partnership tax return in order to avoid costly mistakes.

Pitfalls of Partnerships

Partnership agreements should be formalized in writing and reviewed by a business attorney because they are fraught with problems. A partnership is like being married, but not being in love. There are at least four ways partnerships can cause problems.

1. Business partnerships are easy to get into, but difficult to dissolve. Just like a marriage, partnerships can be very complex with hurt feelings, betrayals, cheating and self-preservation. Sometimes dissolving a partnership is similar to a divorce because of the large amounts of money involved or because the broken relationship ends up destroying the business.

2. Unequal effort and reward. A partnership agreement might state that the profits are split 50/50, but what about equality of the work load or expenses? What if you work more hours than your partner or what if he or she racks up more expenses than you do? These differences can cause a lot of problems. Rarely are partnerships truly an equal division of labor. Usually one person becomes the leader and this can lead to resentment from the other member(s).

3. Debt obligations of others. Like in a marriage, you are responsible for the debts of the other partners while in a

partnership. You have very little recourse if your partner spends freely while you are trying to be frugal.

4. Tied for life. A partnership dissolves when both partners agree or upon the death of a partner. What if you want out of a partnership agreement, but your partner does not? You are stuck unless you are ready to take legal action or offer to buy out your partner.

I usually encourage authors to avoid partnerships. If you are like my client Brent and lack expertise in an area, hire someone to help you. Do not make an employee or independent contractor a business partner. You will be tied together for life.

Avoid entering into a partnership agreement, even on an informal basis. Be very careful about what you agree to or say because even verbal agreements can be binding. Be cautious about using the word partner, when a true partnership does not exist. A new buzz phrase in internet marketing is "joint venture partners." These are not true partnerships, but more of an affiliate or commission-sale working agreement. I dislike the word partnership misused in that way. Authors might believe that partnerships are easy to form and then walk into a true partnership unprepared for the legal and financial entanglements.

Careful Planning

Before you enter into a partnership, even if it just a verbal agreement, discuss with your partners everything that can go wrong.

- Discuss expectations and vision. What does each of you expect to get out of the partnership?
- Evaluate what each partner brings to the table.
- Discuss how to share workload. Who does what?
- Discuss profit sharing. 50/50 rarely works. Ask any business attorney or CPA to advise you about the pitfalls to partnership arrangements so you will be informed. Most likely they

will recommend a 60/40 or alternative split if you decide to proceed with this arrangement.

- Create a budget and financial projection with different scenarios. If you cannot discuss money when there isn't any, it may be difficult to have cool headed discussions when the money starts flowing (or the bills come due).
- Discuss the consequences of one partner failing to carry their share of the workload.
- Consider alternative working arrangements such as employee or independent contractor agreements.

Consider Alternatives

I encourage writers to consider alternative work arrangements instead of forming a partnership. As an author, you might consider hiring help instead of forming a partnership.

Example: Angie had a neat idea for a series of books to help adoptive families learn about their child's country of origin. She was considering a partnership with her sister-in-law. Angie would do the writing and marketing while her sister-in-law did illustrations for the books. I strongly advised Angie to avoid a business partnership, especially with a family member. I was imagining Thanksgiving dinner if something went wrong in the business. Instead, Angie formed a sole proprietorship and hired her sister-in-law as an illustrator and paid her for each book project.

Publishing Contracts

Publishing contracts are a good example of how to structure a business without forming a partnership. I agreed to a publishing contract to write this book with Felice Gerwitz, owner of Media Angels© Inc., but I have not formed a business partnership with Felice. I run my own accounting practice and Felice runs her publishing business. We file separate tax returns and incur our income and expenses separately. Felice and I discussed many aspects of the agreement before she sent me a written contract. Then I had an attorney look over the contract and I spoke to other authors. I wanted to go into our agreement with a clear understanding of what was expected from me and Felice's role as well.

Co-Authors Agreements

Many authors benefit from co-authoring books. They can be great working arrangements with each writer bringing in separate skills. A co-author may be beneficial to you in sharing his or her experiences. I recommend that both authors remain as separate business and not form a business partnership to co-author a book. Each author should have a contract with the publisher that defines responsibilities and compensation. The co-authors work together like employees or co-workers, but they do not have a business partnership structure.

Always have a written agreement with your co-author that outlines royalty sharing, time lines, ownership rights, and other financial arrangements. Michael Lee said it best, "Don't rely on friendship to carry you through lawsuits." To learn from other authors as they share their experiences on co-authoring visit www. speakernetnews.com and search for "co-author."

Perhaps a co-author is not required, but instead a critique partner, an editor or a business mentor would be a better match for your needs. Sometimes a writing teacher or coach can fulfill many more roles for a writer than a co-author. There are many writing forums for authors that allow those with experience to share their talents. You may consider joining one in order to find qualified people with the experience you desire.

In a Nutshell

Partnerships with other authors should be carefully considered. Enter into any agreements with a full understanding of the obligations and responsibilities. Discuss expectations and consequences with potential partners. Put all your agreements in writing and have an attorney look it over and offer advice.

CHAPTER FIVE

CORPORATIONS

I have discussed several common business forms for authors including the popular sole proprietorship and the lesser-used partnerships. A more complicated, but potentially beneficial business structure is the corporation. The main benefit of corporate business status is limited liability for the owners. The corporation offers a shield of protection so that the author's personal assets are protected from business liabilities. Additionally, corporate status may offer some tax benefits for writers and publishers.

Corporations are desirable business structures for authors who form a publishing company, hire employees or do very well financially. I consider "doing well financially" to mean earning at least $50,000 annually or enough to support yourself or your family. Your accountant may define it differently.

There are two types of corporations—S corporations and C corporations. An S corporation is named for a section of the tax code, but I like to think of the S as meaning small. S corporations have a limited number of shareholders (100), so indeed many of them are small corporations, but many times an S corporation has only one shareholder, the owner. On the other hand, C corporations can have an unlimited number of shareholders, are typically run by a board of directors, issue stock and distribute dividends.

S Corporations

If you are considering corporate status for your writing or publishing business, start by learning about S corporations. They may be easier to establish, understand and manage than a C corporation. This is where a tax professional and attorney can be an important asset.

Taxes for S Corporations

S corporations, like partnerships, are "pass through" entities, meaning that all profit or loss is passed to the shareholders and reported on their personal tax returns. An S corporation files a tax return, Form 1120, and each individual shareholder reports their share of income on their own tax returns. The tax preparer for the corporation will issue each shareholder a Form called a K-1 to be used in their individual tax preparation. The tax preparation and record keeping for corporations is quite complicated and expensive.

An author may be advised to create an S corporation to save on self-employment taxes. Self-employment taxes are Social Security and Medicare taxes that self-employed people pay. An employee has half the Social Security and Medicare taxes withheld from his or her paycheck and the employer pays the other half of the tax. Since there is no employee or employer for self-employed people, the owner pays both halves of Social Security and Medicare taxes and it is called self- employment tax. Self-employment tax is approximately 15.3% of the owner's profit.

Usually, an author who forms an S corporation also works in the business providing services. In this situation the owner of the S corp is also an employee of the S corp. The S corporation will provide a paycheck and a W-2 complete with payroll taxes and withholdings to the owner-employee. Therefore, the S corporation pays half of Social Security and Medicare taxes as the employer. The owner-employee has the other half of Social Security and Medicare withheld from his or her paychecks. The full amount of self-employment tax is still paid, half by the corporation and half by the owner-employee.

Sometimes, S corporations save on paying taxes, particularly self-employment tax by taking some of the profit as wages for the owner and some as ordinary income from the business (called "distributions" by the IRS). This is very common with single member S corporation where there are no shareholders. Distributions from an S corporation are not subject to self-employment tax.

Example: Elaine ran her business as a sole proprietorship for many years. Last year she had net income of $50,000. Her tax adviser recommended that she form an S corporation. Elaine determines that she provides services worth $40,000 to her S corporation and takes a salary of $40,000. The remaining portion of $10,000 is from passive income sources and is considered a distribution, not wages. Elaine and the S corporation will pay Social Security and Medicare taxes on only $40,000, not the full $50,000.

Caution on S Corps

A word of caution about S corporations is needed. The Internal Revenue Service (IRS) requires S corporations to pay "reasonable" compensation to an owner who provides services to the S corporation. This compensation is in the form of earned income and is subject to employment taxes (Social Security and Medicare). It would be very common for an author to provide services to her S corporation such as doing the writing and marketing of a book. In fact, almost all the income generated by an author in an S Corp could be considered "active" income because she actually works in the business and is thus subject to employment taxes.

It is more likely that a publishing company may have income that is passive than an author who actively works at writing and marketing his books. Passive income for a publisher includes income from book sales after the initial production work is complete. The passive income could be classified as distributions earned by the corporation. If you form a S corporation, please seek professional accounting advice on determining your compensation as wages and profit distributed as ordinary income.

The IRS may get suspicious if too little money is taken as wages and too much declared as distributions It looks like tax evasion of the employment taxes. Many tax experts think that the IRS may begin to disallow distribution income for S corporations and require all income to be taxed as wages. Indeed, the IRS has increased their audits of S corporations paying below-average or "unreasonable" wages.

> Example: John, an author, provides services to his S corporation including writing, publishing and distributing his books. He is the only employee and sole owner of his S corporation. He has no passive income. All of his profits would be considered "active" income given to John as wages and subject to employment taxes.

Payroll and Tax Preparation for S Corps

As mentioned previously, an S corporation issues a paycheck to the owner-employee who actively works in the corporation as wages for services performed. Employee payroll and tax preparation may be quite a burden for a sole owner of an S corporation. Consider carefully the extra bookkeeping, tax preparation fees and record keeping involved in running a S corporation. Discuss the pros and cons with a knowledgeable CPA.

When to Consider S Corporation Status

❏ You wish limited liability to protect your personal assets
❏ You wish to reduce self-employment taxes because part of your income is from passive sources.
❏ You can pay yourself reasonable compensation from your businesses
❏ You are prepared to deal with the legal and financial complexities of a corporation
❏ You can afford the cost of a business attorney to incorporate your business and a CPA to prepare your payroll and tax preparation.

C Corporations

A corporation that does not elect S corporation status is, by default, a C corporation. C corporations are by far the majority of corporations. The major companies in the world are C corporations.

If you are a solo writer, forming a C corporation may not be part of your plan, because they are overly complex for your needs. Alternatively, if you operate a publishing company, you might consider C corporation status if you have growth plans or need to raise large sums of money. There are several advantages and disadvantages to C corporation status for a publishing company.

Advantages

The greatest advantage corporate status offers is limited liability for the owners. Owners are not personally liable for the company's losses or debts. Their financial risk is limited to what they have invested in the company. Also, corporations find it easier to raise capital though issuing stock (ownership) in the corporation. C corporations are not limited to the number of shareholders as are S corporations. They also offer more choices of stock ownership and structure, such as common and preferred stock. C corporations can also fully deduct most reasonable employee benefit costs, whereas S corporations are more limited.

Disadvantages

C corporations are complex in many ways including structure, taxes and accounting. They require a board of directors, bylaws and formation documents. C corporations also issue stock and must follow many federal and state laws involved in a public offering. Additionally, the accounting system in a publishing corporation can be complex and typically require in-house accounting staff. Ultimately, one grave disadvantage of a corporation is the loss of control. Did you know that General Electric fired their founder, Thomas Edison? It can happen. Unfortunately, just because you started a corporation does not mean that you have complete control. You are subject to the decisions of a board of directors and they work for the shareholders, not you.

Taxes for C Corps

Corporations are subject to federal taxes as a separate entity from their owners. The owners of a corporation are the shareholders and they receive a portion of the profits as dividends. Corporations are subject to what is called "double taxation." The corporation pays taxes and then distributes dividends to shareholders who are taxed on the dividend income. The income tax rate for a corporation may be lower than the tax rates for individuals, but the corporate tax rules are quite complex and you will need the assistance of a qualified CPA to file your C corporation tax returns.

If you form your publishing company as a C corporation, you will typically take a salary as one of the officers. You may also be a major shareholder and collect dividends. You will pay income tax on your salary and dividends from the corporation. Your personal tax return will be separate from the corporation's tax return.

When to Consider C Corporation Status

- You wish limited liability to protect your personal assets
- You wish to reduce self-employment taxes

- You need capital from investors to grow your businesses
- You are prepared to deal with the legal and financial complexities
- You can afford the cost of a business attorney to incorporate your business and a CPA to prepare your payroll and tax preparation.

In a Nutshell

I highly recommend that you consult with several attorneys and CPAs before you consider S or C corporation status. Make sure you understand all advantages and disadvantages of corporate status. Do not rush into any situations that you do not fully understand without good business advice that is in line with your goals.

CHAPTER SIX

LIMITED LIABILITY COMPANIES

I have discussed various for-profit business structures for authors including sole proprietorships, partnerships and corporations. You may have heard about another type of business structure called a Limited Liability Company or LLC. LLCs are a very popular and relatively new business structure, only becoming legal in all 50 states in the 1980s.

Benefits of LLC Status

LLCs can be confusing because they are sometimes thought of as a corporation, but the C in LLC stands for *company,* not corporation. The confusion may come about because LLCs can choose the way they are taxed, as a sole proprietorship, partnership or corporation. Although an LLC is not necessarily a corporation, it does offer several benefits similar to corporations, partnerships and sole proprietorships.

- LLCs offer limited liability protection. Limited liability means that the owners are not personally liable for the debts and liabilities of the business. In this way they are similar to corporations. For example, if an LLC files bankruptcy, the owner will not be required to cover the debts with his or her own money. Alternatively, a sole proprietor is fully responsible for all business debts. Of course, there are situations where an LLC owner can be held liable such as personally guaranteeing a loan, intermingling funds and violating the law. The advantage of limited liability is the main reason why authors and other small business owners choose LLC status for their business.

  Example: A ghost writer was sued for breech of contract. Fortunately, he had limited liability status for his writing business. This protected his personal assets from liability while he fought the lawsuit. Only his business assets were in potential danger. (By the way, he won the lawsuit).

- LLCs are very flexible and can have from one owner to several owners (called "members"). A single member LLC is a sole proprietorship with only one owner.

- An LLC can chose to be taxed as a sole proprietor, partnership, S corporation or C corporation. In other words, you do not cease operating as a sole proprietorship (or partnership or corporation) when you form an LLC.

- An LLC is a separate, distinct legal entity. The LLC owner can open a checking account, obtain a lease and enter into agreements in the name of the LLC and not as an individual.

- LLC is a legal status in your state; it is not a tax status with the IRS. An LLC is a "disregarded entity" for tax purposes meaning that the taxes are reported the same way as before the LLC status was granted. A single member LLC files the same tax return as a sole proprietorship (Schedule C on the Form 1040). A multi-member LLC files either a partnership or corporate income tax return depending on how they are structured.

- LLCs are not subject to double taxation by paying taxes on income and shareholders being taxed on dividends like a corporation. An LLC is what the IRS calls a "pass-through entity." All of the profits and losses of the LLC "pass through" the business to the owners who report this information on their personal tax returns. The LLC itself does not pay federal income taxes, but some states may impose an annual tax.

    True Story: My accounting business, Carol Topp, CPA, was operated as a sole proprietor for its first six years in business. After six years, I was attracting more clients, some from across the country, and I was generating more income. In addition to obtaining professional liability insurance, I formed my business as a single member LLC in my home state by filing the paperwork and paying a $125 fee. My business name is now Carol Topp, CPA, LLC and I still file the Schedule C as a sole proprietor with my Form 1040 tax return and pay self-employment taxes.

Disadvantages of LLC Status

The disadvantages to forming an LLC are small compared to their advantages:

- There is formal paperwork to be filed with your state and an accompanying fee. Oftentimes the paperwork is fairly straightforward, especially for single member

LLCs. Some individuals file for LLC status without assistance, but I always recommend you seek professional advice to understand the pros and cons of LLC for your business. If your LLC has multiple members or is a complex arrangement, you should hire a business attorney to assist you in establishing your LLC.

- Earnings from a single-member LLC are still subject to self-employment taxes, just like a sole proprietorship. Your tax structure does not change by having limited liability status.

- Some states impose franchise tax, an annual registration fee or a renewal fee on LLCs. In most states, the fee is about $100, but California charges a minimum $800 franchise tax per year on LLCs. To determine your state's requirements visit your Secretary of State's website. See the Resources chapter for some helpful websites.

- There are other disadvantages that are specific to partnerships and corporations formed as LLCs. These are beyond the scope of this book. If you are considering a multi-member, partnership or corporate LLC, hire a knowledgeable CPA and business attorney to review the arrangement.

When to Consider Limited Liability Status
- You wish limited liability to protect your personal assets.
- You understand the fees, annual reporting and taxes your state may levy on LLCs.
- You can afford to consult with a business attorney to fully understand the legal implications of LLC status.
- You can afford to hire an attorney to prepare the legal documents, especially if you are forming a multi-member LLC.

In a Nutshell

There is no single best form of ownership for a writing business. The decision will depend on the nature of your work, the income it generates and your personal priorities. You may need to re-evaluate your choice of entity as your business grows. A business attorney or CPA can help you decide which business structure is best for you.

CHAPTER 7

FINANCIAL PLANNING FOR YOUR BUSINESS

Every business book will tell you to create a business plan. This book is no exception. Writing and publishing a book takes a well thought out plan. Most book plans start with a book proposal. If you have not yet drafted your book proposal, read *Information in a Nutshell: Writing and Publishing* by Felice Gerwitz. Felice, an author and publisher, walks you through many of the decisions needed to bring a book to publication. She covers your product (the book's topic), the intended audience, marketing and promotion. After you read through *Writing and Publishing*, you will have your business plan almost complete. Then it is time to complete the final details of your business plan involving the financial details and that topic is covered in this chapter.

Business Plan: Financial Section

A businesses financial plan should have several parts. They follow the chronological progress of writing and publishing a book:

- Start-Up Expenses
- Initial Production Costs
- Break Even Analysis
- Pricing Your Book
- Funding Sources

Start-Up Expenses

Long before you have your book published, you will have incurred some expenses. Record all these expenses and keep your records for several years. Start-up expenses are a tax deduction, so keep good records.

The Internal Revenue Service says that start-up costs include:

- Analyses and surveys of potential markets
- Advertisements announcing the book launch
- Compensation for employees while they are being trained and for their instructors
- Travel and other necessary costs for securing prospective distributors, suppliers or customers
- Professional services for attorneys and accountants
- Corporation or partnership filing fees[2]

In addition, for writers and publishers, start up costs might include:

- Book research including travel, books and reference materials
- Editors, graphic designers, layout designers and indexers
- Website design and set up
- Postage and office supplies to set up your office

Start-up costs do *not* include purchase of equipment or the book production costs; they are considered capital expenses and cost of goods sold, respectively. Your CPA can make the determination for

---

2 www.irs.gov/publications/p535/

you and record start-up expenses properly on your tax return. Your job is to keep good records.

Tax Deduction For Start Up Expenses

The IRS allows small business owners to deduct some or all of their start-up expenses in the first year of operation. In 2010 Congress increased the deduction for start up expenses from $5,000 to $10,000. Any costs not deducted initially may be deducted over a 180-month period, beginning with the month you begin your business. Be sure to tell your tax preparer what expenses are start-up expenses (incurred before your began the business) and what expenses were incurred after you started the business. There are limits on the amount that can be taken as start-up expenses, and the amounts are subject to change, so work closely with a CPA to take the proper tax deduction.

When Does a Business Start?

For many writers and authors, it may not be easy to tell when you business started. A shop owner can name the date he opened his store for business, but writing can be less defined. Here are some guidelines to help you determine when your business was born.

- The date your website goes live
- The date a contract is signed
- The date a book campaign is launched
- The date of your first sale of a book
- The date your book advance check is received
- The date you begin advertising your services as a writer or publisher
- The date you are paid for an article you wrote
- The date of incorporation

Example: Cathy's book has been in the planning stages for several years. Finally this year, she has a book contract. Her publisher will hire an editor and graphic designer, but Cathy knows that a lot of the marketing will be up to her. Because she is a new author, her publisher will not give her an advance, so all the start up expenses are Cathy's responsibility. Fortunately, she kept records of her start-up expenses:

Cathy's Start Up Expenses

Research books and materials	$175.00
Website set up	$350.00
Attorney to set up an LLC	$800.00
Accountant for advice	$300.00
Travel to writers workshops for 3 years	$1,500.00
Printing, brochures, bookmarks, etc.	$400.00
Literary agent fees	$500.00
Total Start-up Expenses	$4,025.00

Cathy gives all this information to her accountant. They will discuss whether Cathy wishes to take a deduction for all the start-up expenses in the first year or spread some of it out (called amortization) for the next 15 years.

Initial Production Costs

In addition to the start-up expenses, many authors find they must also plan for the initial production costs of their book. Naturally if you have a book contract with a publisher, the production costs are paid by the publisher, but many authors prefer to self-publish. To understand the merits and costs of self-publishing read *Information in a Nutshell: Writing and Publishing* by Felice Gerwitz. In this chapter, I will assume that you are a self-publisher and need to calculate initial production costs.

Like start-up costs, book production costs start long before the book is printed. They include pre-production costs such as cover design, copy editors, proof readers, obtaining an ISBN, Library of Congress number and bar code. Additionally, there is the actual cost of printing which can vary depending on size and paper choices.

Finally there are shipping, storage and postage costs or distributor fees if you hire a service to fulfill orders.

Example: Dan decides to self-publish his first book. He plans well and estimates his production costs as the following:

Dan's book production costs

Cover design including bar code	$650.00
Editing and Indexing	$1,200.00
ISBN & LCCN	$350.00
Initial printing of 1,000 copies	$2,550.00
Shipping	$245.00
Mailing 100 copies to reviewers	$450.00
Total initial production (1,000 books)	$5,445.00
Cost per book	$5.45

Planning your initial production costs helps in budgeting these expenses. You may determine you cannot pursue your initial production run until you have the money saved up. Calculating the cost of the initial run will also help in determining a book price and knowing your break-even point, which helps you set sales goals.

Break-Even Analysis

An important part of business planning is to calculate a break-even point. For an author, a break-even point is a simple calculation to determine how many books you need to sell to cover your start up and initial production costs. It is called the break-even point, because you have covered your expenses and are now starting to make a profit.

A break-even point is calculated as:

$$\text{Break-even point (in number of books)} = \frac{\text{Start-up Expenses} + \text{Initial Production Costs}}{\text{Selling price per book}}$$

I will use Dan, the self published author from earlier, to demonstrate a break-even analysis. Dan spent $5,445 to design and print 1,000 copies of his book. He also spend $1,200 in start up expenses for his website, professional advice, research and marketing, making a total investment of $6,645. Dan sells his book for $12.95 and adds on the appropriate sales tax and shipping expenses.

Dan's break-even point = $6,645/ $12.95 per book = 513 books.

After Dan has sold 513 books at $12.95 each, he will have recouped his start up and initial production costs. Any books sold after the first 513 is all profit for Dan.

Doing a break-even analysis can be a great incentive to market and sell your books. It is a goal to strive for as quickly as possible in your book's first year.

Pricing Your Book

When pricing your book, you should consider several factors:
- Your production costs. Some experts recommend you price your book at 5 to 8 times the cost to print the book.
- Your start-up costs which you wish to recoup as soon as possible.
- Ability to discount your book and still cover your costs. Distributors, booksellers and Amazon all expect steep discounts from author/self-publishers of 50-67%.
- Retail price of competing books. Overcharging what the market can bear will reduce your sales even if your book is better than the competition.

Calculate your sale price several different ways and then do a market survey of potential buyers. See what they would be willing to pay for your book.

Example: John tries several methods to determine a book selling price. He pays $2.80 to have the book printed and finds competing books sell for $14.95. He wishes to recoup his start-up and initial production costs of $8,000 by selling 500 books.

- Printing cost method (5 to 8 times the cost to print the book): $2.80 * 5 = $14.00 per book; $2.80 * 8 = $22.40 per book
- Recoup start-up and initial production costs: $8,000/ 500 books = $16.00 per book
- Discount method: John could set his retail price at $15.00 and offer a 60% discount making the cost to a bookstore = $9.00, leaving John $6.00 to cover printing and other expenses.
- Competitor price: $14.95

This gives John some ideas that his book should probably be priced form $14.95 to $22.40 per book.

Funding Start-Up and Initial Production Costs

As you can imagine, start-up costs can add up quickly. Most authors lay out all or most of the start-up expenses themselves, unless they are awarded an advance from their publisher. There are a few options to finance your book including using your savings, obtaining a loan or going into debt. I do not recommend taking out a loan or using your credit card to finance your book. Publishing can be a risky business and the royalties or sales from your book may never amount to much. It is sad to say, but you may not have financial success with writing and may be unable to repay the loan or credit card debt.

Instead of using debt, I recommend you save up as much as possible beforehand. Plan carefully how much you will need in start up expenses. Shop frugally for everything from editors to ink to keep your expenses low. Do as much as you can yourself, learn a lot and grow slowly. Many business owners start with very little and only grow their business as the profits increase.

In a Nutshell

Creating a business plan for your book includes doing several financial projections including:
- Start-up expenses
- Initial production costs
- Break-even analysis
- Pricing your book
- Funding sources

Failure to plan is planning to fail, so create a financial plan for your book and you will increase the chances of your business being successful.

CHAPTER 8

ORGANIZING BUSINESS RECORDS

Financial records are extremely important to successfully running a writing or publishing business. I think that the simplest system works best. In this and the next two chapters, I will share some basic tips for record keeping. I cover what records to keep, how to get organized, how to record transactions and when software might be helpful. Start simple and gradually grow in your record keeping as your writing business grows.

I recommend that you start with a simple file folder system to organize your business records. You may wish to buy an expandable file folder or use a file drawer with individual folders. These folders have three main purposes:

- Organize the written records of your income and expenses
- Organize all your banking records including credit cards and Paypal statements
- Maintain records on official correspondence with state and federal governments

Records of Income and Expenses

Income

You may wish to file all written evidence of your income into one folder. File all sales receipts, royalty payments, paid invoices from clients and income statements from Paypal or your website shopping cart. If your business is very active, you might wish to have several folders for your various types of income.

Here's a tip regarding bank deposit slips: Write the source of the income on the deposit slip itself. When I deposit checks from various clients, I write the client's name on the deposit slip. I used to receive a carbon-less copy of my deposit slip from the bank. It was an excellent record keeping system for me. Now, my bank allows me to see my deposit slips on-line, so I still record the client's name on the deposit slip.

Expenses

Expenses are usually more complex than income and I recommend that you devote several folders to sort expenses by categories. To make tax preparation simpler, use categories that correspond to the sole proprietorship business tax return, Schedule C Profit or Loss from Business. Even if you are not a sole proprietor, these are still the recommended categories for filing your business expenses. Chapter 13 Income Tax for Authors covers the Schedule C and these business expenses in more detail.

- Advertising. This should include your website fees.
- Transportation. Keep a log of your business miles. The IRS requires a written record; estimates of mileage will not suffice.
- Equipment and software purchases
- Professional fees to accountants and lawyers
- Contract labor to hire professionals such as editors, web designers, etc.
- Office supplies
- Purchase of items for resale (i.e., inventory)

- Shipping supplies
- Utilities including your cell phone and internet bills. These should be prorated for business use only on the tax return.
- Wages paid to employees and payroll taxes
- Other expenses including bank, merchant and Paypal fees as well as professional development expenses for books, magazines or conferences.

In each folder store your receipts, paid bills, sales slips or whatever proof you have of business expenses.

Banking Records

In another group of folders organize your bank statements, deposit slips and charge card statements.

Credit Cards and Paypal Statements

I prefer to think of credits cards as another bank account and so the credit card statements are filed in their own folder, in the banking portion of your file system. The same is true of Paypal or other on-line payment systems or shopping carts. Paypal is really just a type of bank account. Have a folder labeled Paypal and make monthly print outs of your Paypal activity. Although, we are quickly becoming a paperless society, the IRS still requires written proof of business income and expenses, so use your printer and keep paper copies.

Checkbook Tips

Although you do not need to file your checkbook itself into a folder, have a place for the important documents related to the account. I highly recommend a separate business checking account. Keep a separate checking account for your writing business, and use it only for business expenses, not personal spending. When you wish to withdraw money for personal use, write a check to yourself or transfer funds into your personal checking account and then spend the money from your personal account. It might be easier to just use the business debit card at the grocery store, but co-mingling of funds will become confusing at tax time. It can be expensive, too, if your CPA spends valuable time sorting individual transactions into business and personal expenses.

I also recommend duplicate checks. They provide a written record of expenses. Many banks no longer return canceled checks and many are not keeping electronic backups for more than a year.

Government Correspondence

Keep copies of *everything* you mail to the IRS and to state and city governments. File away copies of all forms and checks you write to pay taxes (or use duplicate checks). Save every letter sent to or received from any government agency, especially confirmation of your EIN (Employer Identification Number), vendor licenses and name registration. You may need several folders for this section, depending on your business size and structure.

Your files will be well organized if you have folders for income, expenses, banking, and government correspondence. Now you will need a simple flow chart of the process to record your business transactions and keep your filing system organized.

Record Keeping Process

- Pay your expenses from your business checking account via a check or debit card.
- Regularly enter these transactions into your bookkeeping system. (I cover bookkeeping systems in the next two chapters). Some authors find that they only need to enter transactions once a month. Other authors or publishers set aside time once a week to enter transactions. Large businesses may hire a bookkeeper to enter the transactions.
- File the receipts into the expenses folders after they have been entered into your bookkeeping system.

- Enter your income into your bookkeeping system when it is received. File proof of income such as the pay stubs from royalty checks into your income folder. File deposit slips into your banking folder.
- Balance your business checking account monthly. After the account has been balanced, file the bank statements into the correct banking folder.
- Once a year, gather the paperwork from the income and expenses folders for your tax preparer. After the tax return has been completed, store the papers in a large envelope labeled with the proper year. Retain these receipts for at least three years; seven years is recommended. You may also wish to store your bank statements in envelopes labeled by year and retain them for at least three years. The government correspondence records should stay in your file folder system permanently.

In A Nutshell

Benjamin Franklin is credited with saying, "A place for everything and everything in its place." This is good advice for all small business owners. Keep your business records organized in a file folder system. Do an annual clean up by storing all documents in envelopes labeled by year. Retain these envelopes for at least three years. You will be very happy that you stayed organized at tax time or if you need to retrieve an important document.

CHAPTER 9

A SIMPLE BOOKKEEPING METHOD

For many busy writers record keeping can become an unnecessary ordeal. With some advanced planning this can easily be avoided. I recommend that authors keep their system as simple as possible and expand their bookkeeping needs as their business grows. The system described here uses single entry bookkeeping, not double entry bookkeeping that is taught to accountants. Record keeping can be easily recorded on paper, in a spreadsheet program or on a computer.

There are only three steps involved in setting up a bookkeeping system.

Step 1: Set Up

- Divide a sheet of paper into columns or use a columnar sheet sold at office supply stores. Some writers prefer graph paper or create a spreadsheet on the computer.
- Label the columns *Date*, *Check Number*, *Description* and

Income and leave several columns for expenses.

- Label each page with the current month. If using a spreadsheet, use a different tab for each month.

Step 2: Recording

Record your income in one column and expenses in several other columns. Record every transaction whether from the checking account, credit card or cash. Keep up with this step at least monthly or weekly if your business is active. At the end of every month, total each income and expense column.

Below is an example of an author's business transactions for one month. Your columns for expenses may differ from this example. If you have several columns for expenses you may wish to turn the page horizontally, or use a computer spreadsheet.

Month of: January

Date	Check Number	Description	Income	Advertising	Office	Postage	Meals	Mileage
1/09/200X	Debit card	Website fee		S 20.00				
1/10/200X		Income from book sales	$ 250.00					
1/11/200X	203	Ink			$12.00			
1/15/200X	204	Brochures		S 32.00				
1/15/200X	cash	Lunch with Client B					S 8.50	
		Mileage to lunch meeting(round trip)						12
1/30/200X	205	Stamps				$ 55.00		
1/30/200X		Mileage to post office						6
Totals			$ 250.00	$52.00	$12.00	$ 55.00	$ 8.50	18

Step 3: Summary Spreadsheet

Every month, carry the totals for that month to a summary sheet. This sheet will summarize your business performance every month. A quick glance at your summary sheet will reveal your major expenses. It will also show you whether there is a profit, a loss, or if you broke even. This summary spreadsheet also makes tax preparation easy since all the expenses are in categories with totals.

Below is an example of a summary spreadsheet kept in Open Office Calculate (a free spreadsheet program virtually identical to Microsoft Excel). The total income and expense columns for the first three months are shown. For the first quarter of the year, this business owner can see that her income was $3,100 and her total expenses were $512.

If you are good with a spreadsheet, you can create this summary spreadsheet automatically with some copy and paste commands and avoid retyping the data. Perhaps a bookkeeper, virtual assistant or accountant can set up a bookkeeping spreadsheet for you.

SmallBusinessBookkeeping.xls - OpenOffice.org Calc

File Edit View Insert Format Tools Data Window Help

	B	C	D	E	F	G	H	I	J
1	Month	Income	Advertising	Office Supplies	Postage	Meals	Total Expenses	Purchased Inventory	Miles
2	January	$250.00	$52.00	$12.00	$55.00	$8.50	$87.00	$0.00	18
3	February	$1,200.00	$75.00	$0.00	$0.00		$75.00	$500.00	10
4	March	$1,650.00	$50.00	$150.00	$150.00		$350.00	$0.00	65
5									
6	Total	$3,100.00	$177.00	$162.00	$205.00	$8.50	$512.00	$500.00	93
7									

January / February / March \ Summary /

On the spreadsheet above, you will notice an additional column for purchased inventory. It is a separate column from other expenses because inventory is handled differently from other business expenses for tax purposes. The United States tax system allows authors and publishers to deduct only the portion of inventory that is sold each year, not the full purchased amount. This deduction for the books actually sold is called Cost of Goods Sold. Inventory and Cost of Goods Sold are discussed in Chapter 11.

This example spreadsheet also displays mileage in a column. Your tax preparer will apply the correct mileage deduction in dollars on your tax return if you supply the total number of business miles driven in a year. The Internal Revenue Service sets a mileage rate for business deductions and it can change frequently—usually once a year. In 2010 the rate was $.50 per mile. In 2011 the rate will be $.51 per mile.

In A Nutshell

Record keeping can be done on paper or on an electronic spreadsheet. I have small business clients that use both quite successfully. If you find your writing business growing, you may wish to use software to manage the bookkeeping. The next chapter discusses some software options.

CHAPTER TEN

RECORD KEEPING WITH SOFTWARE

There are a variety of software programs available to help authors and publishers handle their bookkeeping. They range from general purpose money management software to very specific applications designed to manage inventory and royalty payments. Pick a system that is easy for you to understand and advance to more sophisticated software when your business grows.

Personal Money Management Software

If your writing business is small enough, a paper or spreadsheet record keeping system explained in Chapter Nine will usually suffice, but some writers find computer software to be very useful. Many authors find that personal money management software can work well for record keeping. Some of the most popular money management programs include Quicken, Mint.com, an on-line service and GnuCash, a free, open-source porgram. Although these programs are not designed for business use, they can be very simple to learn. All generate simple reports showing income and expenses.

> Example: Cindy used Quicken to manage her personal finances. She authored articles for magazines and was paid well. She created an income category called "Writing Income" in Quicken. She also created expense categories called "Writing: Office Supplies" and "Writing: Research" for her writing business. At the end of the year, it was simple to get Quicken to generate a report showing her total income and expenses from writing.

See the Resources chapter for a listing of personal money management tools and an updated list at this book's website, TaxesForWriters.com.

Accounting Software

There are times when personal money management software like Quicken or Mint.com may not be enough to manage your writing business. Then you will need small business accounting software. There are several programs to chose from. The most popular is QuickBooks, but other packages include Peachtree Accounting and several new, online services such as Freshbooks.com and Outright.com. Many of the newer, on-line versions are designed for freelancers or micro business owners and have only the essential features an author might need. The market for easy-to-manage business software is growing rapidly and in the future you will find many more options to meet your needs.

See the Resources chapter and TaxesForWriters.com for updates of small business accounting software options.

Accounting software works better than personal money management software if you send your customers invoices, create statements for progress billing, or if you manage inventory.

Accounting software can:

- Print checks, pay bills, track sales and expenses
- Reconcile bank accounts
- Create estimates, invoices and reports
- Track employee time and calculate payroll withholding
- Generate reports such as a profit and loss statement
- Download credit card and bank transactions
- Track inventory and set reorder points
- Create business plans, budgets and forecasts

Example: Cindy continued to use Quicken until she wrote a book and paid for several hundred copies to be printed. She needed to deal with customer orders, invoices and inventory. She now needed small business accounting software, such as QuickBooks.

Several Versions of Software

The most popular small business accounting software is QuickBooks, which comes in several variations depending on your business needs. They offer Mac and PC versions, an on-line version and software for single or multiple users. QuickBooks Pro is a popular version and a good place to start for most authors. The Pro version typically sells for around $200.

You can view a comparison chart of the various QuickBooks versions at http://quickbooks.intuit.com/

True Story: In the beginning of my accounting business, I recorded my income and expenses on paper for three years. I used a columnar pad that I bought for $1.99 at an office supply store. I summarized the paper records into personal finance software, Quicken, and had two general categories: "Carol's Business Income" and "Business Expense." At that time all my income was from preparing tax returns which were paid on delivery, so I never had to invoice a client and I had no inventory. Record keeping was simple. After five years, I grew to add a few small business clients that needed to be billed or were paying in installments, so I switched to QuickBooks Pro so I could prepare and track invoices. Now I have inventory (a few books), sales tax (on my book sales), and I invoice more clients. QuickBooks is now an indispensable tool for me.

Warning About Software

Any accounting software is a wonderful tool, *if* you use it correctly. Please spend the time and money to get your software set up properly and be trained in how to use it. I have met authors that have paid a lot of money to have their QuickBooks records fixed because they set up the software incorrectly. The software is only as good as the information you enter into it. If you enter your data in the incorrect place, QuickBooks cannot fix it for you. As the saying goes, "Garbage in, garbage out."

Intuit, the creators of QuickBooks, has a program called QuickBooks ProAdvisor to help users find local certified professionals (See the Resources chapter or TaxesForWriters.com for website links). These QuickBooks professionals can set up the software, train you and troubleshoot problems. Once an author has been trained, most can do their own data entry and only occasionally (quarterly or annually) meet with an accountant.

Hiring Help with Bookkeeping

There may be times when your business does so well, that the bookkeeping becomes very time consuming. You may wish to hire a bookkeeper to enter transactions so that you can focus on writing.

Example: My friend, Linda, an author, called me asking for bookkeeping help. Orders for her books were very strong and Linda was spending precious time doing data entry into QuickBooks. She was not a numbers person and found that the bookkeeping was distracting her from researching and writing her next book. Linda hired my teenage daughter, Emily, to do data entry into QuickBooks. Emily had a natural knack for numbers and organization that Linda lacked and did the work in half the time it took Linda. Everyone was thrilled with the arrangement. First I fixed some of Linda's QuickBooks accounts because of errors she had made in her setup and in recording transactions. Emily then took over the bookkeeping tasks and met monthly with Linda.

Software For Publishers

Record keeping for publishers can be more complex than for authors because of the royalty payments. Authors depend upon their publishers to keep accurate records of sales and royalty payments. There are a few software packages to help publishers with record keeping:

EasyRoyaltiesUSA.com approximate cost $500

AnyBook Publishers Business Kit offers two versions, Classic for the new business ($39-$89) and Professional (with 6 levels of enhanced features from $89-$649). Both versions generate invoices, manage inventory, calculate royalty payments, and create reports.

Bookmaster has several modules to handle all aspects of a publishing business including royalties, book productions, sales and returns.

The Resources chapter lists website links to these software packages and this book's website, TaxesForWriters.com, has an up-to-date list of software for publishers.

In A Nutshell

As your writing business grows, you may find software very helpful. Your choices are personal money management software such as Quicken, or accounting software such as QuickBooks. QuickBooks comes in several versions and is a wonderful tool if used correctly, so get some professional assistance in the setup and initial training.

Chapter 11

Inventory

If you are like most writers, you probably have a book inside of you waiting to emerge. Whether you capture the attention of a publisher or self-publish, all authors usually keep an inventory of their books nearby. I used a print-on-demand publisher for one of my books, but I still keep a small inventory of 20 to 30 copies in my office at all times. Other authors order large print runs and sell their books from their inventory stock.

This chapter is devoted to an issue faced by every author with a published title: dealing with inventory. Inventory can present several challenges to an author, but inventory records are important for business success and for tax preparation.

Problems With Inventory

Inventory can be one of the most difficult aspects of an author's business for several reasons.

Cost

Unless you work with a publisher or your books are printed on demand, you will need to outlay a sizable amount of money to have your books printed. Many self-published authors try to buy as many books as they can afford because small print runs can be expensive. The larger the volume, the lower the price per unit. Would you rather pay $2.50 per book and buy 1,000 or pay $.50 per book and purchase 4,000 copies? This is a difficult decision. You may be uncertain of how many copies you can sell, and do not want to over-buy.

To make the decision a bit easier, consider carefully the number of books you expect to sell in the first year and have no more than that printed. Dan Poynter, author of *The Self Publishing Manual* recommends no more than 500 copies for your first print run.

"It's better to sell out and have to go back to press quickly than to find yourself with a garage full of unsold books. You'll be spending a lot of money on promotion, so it's best to hedge your bets by tying up less money in the book—even though you have to pay a premium in printing costs to do so." (*Dan Poynter's Self Publishing Manual* by Dan Poynter. p. 144) [My publisher interviewed Dan Poynter and this audio is available on her website at www.InformationInANutshell.com]

Storage

If you print a large amount of books, they need to be stored. Many first time authors use their own home or garage. Some rent a storage unit or add on to their home to accommodate the storage and shipping of their books. Either way, books take up a lot of space, are quite heavy and they need dry, cool places.

Damaged Goods and Returns

If you do your own shipping you will eventually deal with damaged goods or a returned product. Handle all returns or complaints promptly and politely. Remember that the customer is always right. Sometimes a damaged book can be offered to customers at a reduced price.

Shipping

You may want to start your business by shipping books yourself. This will involve:

- receiving the orders, typically via an electronic shopping cart on your website,
- packaging the order,
- printing a label and
- getting the package to the post office or delivery service.

If your orders are small or infrequent, you might find filling orders as an enjoyable way to respond to your customers.

On the other hand, processing orders and shipping books can take over your life. Many busy authors will hire family members to help in the business. Hiring your kids is a great way to run a home-based, family business. Cindy Rushton of CindyRushton.com ran her book publishing business from her home for many years. Her son, Matthew, was in charge of the shipping department until he left home to join the Army. It was when her shipping department literally "shipped out" that Cindy converted to all digital products.

Several other authors shared these tips for running your own shipping department:

- Get a toll free number or use an answering machine to receive orders by phone.
- Create a website and use an electronic shopping cart.
- Accept credit cards or use Paypal.
- Use software such as QuickBooks to record sales, print receipts and manage inventory levels.
- Keep copies of all orders.
- Print out sales receipts that can double as shipping labels.

- Communicate frequently to your customer concerning returns, refunds and back orders.
- Leave the books in their original boxes for easier counting and storage.
- Set up a mailing station near your inventory with all the necessary boxes, tape and packing supplies.
- Visit the post office and UPS in person or online to research various shipping rates and plans.

Alternatives to Shipping Yourself

Instead of running a shipping department yourself, you can use an order fulfillment center. These businesses will warehouse your books, take the orders, package and ship them. Two examples are www.BookMasters.com and BCH Fulfillment & Distribution at www.BookCH.com. You may wish to try smaller distributors and a good book consultant can help you with little known resources. My publisher is a book consultant, and an excellent choice, but there are many others. Again, research and do your homework.

Alternatives to Inventory

Another alternative to buying and shipping inventory is to use a print on demand service (POD). These services print your book one at a time when they are ordered from major on-line book sellers such as Amazon. They also take care of the shipping and payment process. The entire process is invisible to you the author. A POD will allow you to focus on writing and marketing, but your profits will be smaller. PODs can be a feasible alternative for a new author, a writer with a narrow niche or an author willing to do marketing.

Some PODs are:
- Lightning Source
- Xlibris
- iUniverse

- Lulu.com
- CreateSpace (owned by Amazon.com)
- Aventine Press for Christian markets

Their services and prices vary, so take time to compare the alternatives especially in light of the large investment some of these require. On the internet you may find several comparison charts. While they are helpful, they can become dated quickly as new providers enter the POD market. They are valuable to help you consider all the factors if you are considering using a POD printer.

Publisher's Note:

Personally I am not a fan of the Print-on-Demand services of many popular companies, even if I understand why most first time or new authors would choose this method of printing. The main reason is the cost of goods sold. If you plan to make your book available widely through distribution channels such as resellers the book will be too costly to make a good profit. I prefer other channels such as smaller companies that can provide wonderful services and handle fulfillment for the author at a minimal charge. I do use print on demand for specific purposes such as to print a short run, one book at a time or backlisted books. In my experience many authors are unable to recoup the expenses expended using a print on demand service. Another concern is the idea that you will have help in getting your book to print, however I have witnessed book runs with many errors that were unable to be sold, none which were caught by the POD service or the inexperienced author. Be aware that the final review is up to the self-published author and use help in reviewing the sample copy before giving your approval.

Electronic Books

Other authors are turning to electronic books and not printing physical books at all. There are certainly advantages for an author in electronic books. There is no inventory to manage, no printing costs, no storage space needed and no shipping costs. The disadvantages include reader reluctance to purchase ebooks (although this is rapidly changing), lack of bookstore sales, and the pride in seeing your book in actual print.

Most ebooks work well for small books of under 100 pages, without color or illustrations. These books usually cater to a specific niche where the reader wants instant information and seem to be more popular with nonfiction titles than with fiction. Many authors and publishers think that the electronic book will revolutionize the publishing industry. Perhaps it is an alternative that may work for you.

All major publishers and many of the PODs listed above offer electronic delivery of your book as well as print versions. The introduction of ebook readers such as the Kindle and the Nook has helped the ebook market grow quickly. Services to help convert your book to e-reader formats are available. Websites such as Smashwords. com can help convert your book into various electronic formats. You may also hire a professional with access to software and the ability to transfer your book into the popular e-versions. This is a onetime expense instead of an ongoing expense of a service such as Smashwords.com.

Importance of Inventory Control

- Do you know which of your books sells best?
- What inventory should you take to a trade show?
- Which of your books is the most profitable for you?

These questions can be answered with a good inventory tracking system. I highly recommend a small business accounting software package like QuickBooks to manage inventory records. You will need the QuickBooks Pro version or higher to be able to input inventory. See Chapter Ten on software solutions for authors.

You will want to stay abreast of your inventory levels. The goal of inventory is not too much and not too little. Too much inventory leads to cash flow problems. If all your cash has been spent to buy the inventory that remains unsold you may not have the resources for marketing. You may have heard small business owners say, "All my cash is tied up in inventory."

Too little inventory and you may run out of books. Customers often become impatient and may cancel their order or demand a refund if you cannot deliver promptly. Avoid too much or too little inventory by keeping your inventory records up to date. Order only what you need, just before you need it.

Tax Aspects of Inventory

I was preparing a tax return for a small business client, Marianne, when she handed over her receipts for purchases of inventory. They totaled $1,200. "How much of this inventory do you have left?" I asked. She had no idea. She was confused when I explained that she could not deduct all $1,200, but only the portion of the inventory that she sold. I introduced her to a new phrase, *Cost of Goods Sold*.

Cost of Goods Sold (COGS) includes both the cost of the merchandise from the supplier (typically your printer or your publisher) and the shipping cost to get the books delivered to you.

Knowing your cost of goods sold is important for several reasons:

- COGS is a tax deduction. It is put on the Schedule C Profit or Loss from Business and is the first business deduction listed on the form.
- Knowing the cost of your books can help you plan for future purchases. If you know what you paid to order 250 books, you can plan for your next purchase.
- Knowing your cost of goods sold helps you set a profitable selling price. You must cover your costs to purchase the inventory and then add in a mark-up for taxes, overhead and profit.

Cost of Goods Sold

You need several pieces of information to calculate the cost of goods sold:

- Your inventory value at the beginning of the year
- All the purchases or additions you made to your inventory during the year
- The value of your inventory at the end of the year. This involves making a count of your inventory near the end of the year.

The formula used to compute cost of goods sold is:

Cost of Good Sold = Beginning inventory + Purchases added during the year – Inventory at end of the year

Beginning inventory
+ Additions during the year
Goods available for sale
- Year-end inventory
Cost of goods sold

So to continue my example of Marianne, she counted her ending inventory and calculated its value as $650. Her opening inventory was zero since this was her first year in business. So her cost of goods sold is:

Cost of Goods Sold. = $0 (Beginning inventory) + $1,200 (Purchases added during the year) – $650 (Inventory at end of the year) = $550

Beginning inventory	$ 0
+ Additions during the year	$1,200
goods available for sale	$1,200
- Year-end inventory	$ 650
cost of goods sold	$ 550

Marianne included $550 as cost of goods sold on her tax return. Chapter Thirteen covers the tax return for authors in detail.

Counting Inventory

Software systems like QuickBooks can do an excellent job of calculating the value of your inventory, but I recommend making an inventory count at the end of the year for several reasons:

- You may have lost some books or, heaven forbid, have some stolen from you.
- You may need to remove some books from inventory due to damage.
- You may have given away several free copies for reviews and promotions.
- Mistakes can happen.

Some authors or publishers count inventory more frequently than once a year. Counting after a convention, book fair or event is highly recommended. One very busy author was selling her books at a new convention nearly every week of the year and she counted inventory *every week*. Your local accountant can advise you on how frequently you should be counting inventory.

Estimates of ending inventory are not allowed on a tax return, any more than estimates of mileage or expenses are allowed. You must keep accurate records and report true figures.

In A Nutshell

Inventory management is vital to a business' success both financially and for customer service. Unfortunately, inventory management can become an overwhelming task and has problems of cost, storage and shipping. There are several alternatives to storing inventory and doing shipping yourself including using order fulfillment services, print on demand and electronic books. The record keeping and counting of inventory is important for tax purposes and to manage your business for profitability.

CHAPTER 12

SALES TAX

Have you ever thought of yourself as a government agent? You are if you sell a product to the public and add on sales tax. Small business owners act as an agent of their state government when they collect sales tax. Whenever a writer sells a product, such as a book or CD, sales tax must usually be added to the sales price. The author is doing the state's job in collecting the sales tax and then paying the tax to the state, usually monthly or quarterly.

Sales tax laws vary greatly by state and sometime by county or city, so to understand your sales tax obligation you should visit your state's sales tax website. This site links you to tax laws for your state: www.taxadmin.org/fta/link/.

Here is some basic information that pertains to all states regarding collecting and paying sales tax.

How to Keep Sales Tax Records

My recommendation is to keep sales tax record keeping as simple as possible. Keep records of all your sales, both taxable and nontaxable (I'll discuss when you do not have to collect sales tax later). A receipt book is a good idea if you sell your books face-to-face at book tables, fairs or conventions. At the end of the event, total your sales and calculate the sales tax owed.

Here's an example of a sale of two books to a customer with the sales tax clearly shown.

Sales Receipt

Salesperson *Abby Author*	Date	
Qty.	**Item/Description**	**Price/Unit**	**Total**
2	*Best selling book*	$12.95	$25.90
	Subtotal	$25.90
	Sales Tax(6%)	$1.55
	Total	$27.45

Another easy way to keep track of sales is to count your books before and after an event. In the example below, the author sold three types of books. She recorded her beginning inventory for each book. At the end of the event, she counted what remained of each book. By knowing the selling price for each book, she calculates that she started the event with $1,345.00 in inventory and ended with $308.80 in inventory, making her total sales $1,036.20 ($1,345.00 - $308.80). This author will pay sales tax on her sales of $1,036.20.

Event Name	Book Event
Date	

Inventory

Item Name	Price/ Unit	Beginning Qty	Total Beginning Value	Ending Qty	Total Ending Value	Total Sold	Total Sales
Book # 1	$10.95	25	$273.75	7	$76.65	18	$197.10
Book # 2	$8.95	50	$447.50	12	$107.40	38	$340.10
Book # 3	$24.95	25	$623.75	5	$124.75	20	$499.00
Total			$1,345.00		$308.80		$1,036.20

A spreadsheet can be very helpful in recording sales figures and calculating your sales tax. Spreadsheets can be kept on paper, but computer spreadsheets make data entry easy and fast. Microsoft Excel is an extremely popular spreadsheet program. Open Office Calc is a nearly-identical competitor to Excel and it is free from OpenOffice.org.

If you are selling a variety of books and processing many orders, I highly recommend that you use accounting software such as QuickBooks. It will help you track inventory and keep records of sales tax collected and payable. You can even set up the software to remind you to make your sales tax payments to your state. I discuss accounting software in Chapter Ten.

Sales Tax Included in the Price or Not?

I sell one of my books at conventions for an even dollar amount of $10.00 with sales tax included. Fellow author, Linda Hobar, sells her books for $32 and then adds sales tax on top of that price. Which method is better? Should you include the sales tax in the price or should you add it on as an additional cost?

I include sales tax in my price to make it easier on my customers when I sell face-to-face. They are buying a low priced item and are usually paying in cash or by check. To add on 6% or 7% sales tax to a $10 item would mean the customer must hunt up an additional $.60 or $.70. Instead, I really charge $9.43 for the book and charge the customer an additional $.57 in sales tax ($9.43 * 6% = $0.57). I have to do a bit of math after the sale to separate my gross sales from the sales tax collected, but it is not difficult to figure it out.

My sales price including sales tax is $10.00 and my sales tax rate is 6%.

First, I calculate the price of the book *without* tax:
Price without sales tax = Sales Price with sales tax/(1 + sales tax rate)
Price without sales tax = $ 10.00/ (1.06) = $9.43 per book

Then, I can calculate the sales tax:

Sales Tax = Sales Price including sales tax - Price without sales tax
Sales Tax = $ 10.00 - $9.43 = $0.57 for each book.

You can simply substitute your sales price and tax rate to calculate the portion of your total sales that are from sales tax.

I sell at speaking events, conventions and occasionally to individuals. I pay sales tax semi-annually, so I record sales at each event and then calculate the sales tax due from each event. In July, I will pay my state government $55.47 of sales tax on $980.00 of sales. (again, a computer spreadsheet is very useful!)

Event	Date	Total collected	Tax Rate	Book Portion	Sales Tax Portion
Speaking Event	2/7/20XX	$100.00	6.00%	$94.34	$5.66
Convention	3/1/20XX	$120.00	6.00%	$113.21	$6.79
Sales to friend	3/5/20XX	$10.00	6.00%	$9.43	$0.57
Speaking Event	4/1/20XX	$350.00	6.00%	$330.19	$19.81
Convention	5/10/20XX	$400.00	6.00%	$377.36	$22.64
Totals		$980.00		$924.53	$55.47

My customers seem to appreciate the convenience of a nice round number. Linda, on the other hand, has a more expensive book and she is paid by credit card or check and rarely in cash. She creates a receipt for each customer totaling all their sales and then adds on the sales tax. After the convention, it is easy for her to total her gross sales separately from the sales tax she collected.

Event
Date

	Sales (from receipt book)	Sales Tax (from receipt book)	Total Collected	Payment Type
Customer # 1	$32.00	$1.92	$33.92	Visa
Customer # 2	$37.00	$2.22	$39.22	check
Customer # 3	$64.00	$3.84	$67.84	Mastercard
Customer # 4	$32.00	$1.92	$33.92	check
Total	$165.00	$9.90	$174.90	

Linda's spreadsheet also lets her see total sales by payment type. She can determine which payment method is most popular and it serves as a good cross reference to check deposit slips (for checks and cash) and the total payments processed through credit cards.

What method you choose, including sales tax or adding it on, depends upon

- your price
- selling style
- method of payment
- convenience to your customer

Neither method is right or wrong, but you must calculate your gross sales and the sales tax collected correctly.

Making Payments to Your State Government

Before you collect or pay sales tax to your state, you should apply for a seller's permit, sometimes called a vendor's license. Many states ask for sales tax collections to be remitted twice a year, or every six months. Some states want sales tax paid quarterly and if your business is quite large, sales tax must be submitted more frequently such as monthly or weekly. You will need to check your state to see their requirements.

While some states will mail you the paperwork to file your sales tax, many are going paperless and ask business owners to file and pay their sales tax on-line. In my home state of Ohio, businesses are required to file sales tax paperwork on-line. Payment can be made electronically or by mailing a check.

File the Form Even if No Tax is Owed

Some states require the paperwork even if you do not owe any sales tax. One of my clients did not file a sales tax return because he had not made taxable sales for a six month period. He was fined for not filing a sales tax return, even though he did not owe any sales tax. He managed to talk them out of the fine, but it was not easy!

Do Not Spend the Sales Tax Collected

It is very important that you set aside collected sales tax payments and do not spend them on your business. You may even want to keep sales tax payments in a separate bank account. Remember that not all the money in your bank account is yours to spend, some of it goes to the state for sales tax payments.

True Story: Larry became an almost overnight success as an author. His sales went through the roof and he was thrilled until he realized he forgot to set aside a reserve to pay his sales taxes. This was a new experience for him, never having to deal with collecting or paying sales tax in the past he was unprepared. With his newfound success came an increase of income and related taxes. Larry called me after the fact. Unfortunately, he had to borrow money to pay his tax bills. A local CPA can be invaluable in helping you to plan for your sales tax payments.

Exemptions to Sales Tax

There are several circumstances where you can sell your books or products and not collect sales tax. The most common exemptions to sales tax are:

- Selling to someone other than the end user. Generally, states only tax sales on the final user, so if you are selling your books to a bookstore or catalog, you do not charge them sales tax. The store or catalog will collect sales tax from the final purchaser. How do you know if a customer is the final user? Customers who intend to resell your books should present you with a resale certificate or a wholesaler license.

- Selling to a nonprofit organization. In some states, nonprofit organizations are able to obtain sales tax exemption. These organizations should show you a sales tax exemption certificate from their state. If they do not have a sales tax exemption certificate, then you should charge them sales tax. Not all states offer sales tax exemptions to nonprofits and not all nonprofits are eligible for sales tax exemption, so ask for the certificate.

- Selling to out-of-state customers. Usually you must collect sales tax from customers that live in your state, but you do *not* have to collect sales tax from out-of-state customers. This principle is based on what is known as nexus. Nexus means to have a physical presence such as a store, office, employees or a salesman in that state. If you have a nexus in a state, you must collect sales tax in that state. No nexus, then no sales tax. The concept of nexus comes from American history and our Constitution where states were not allowed to tax an out-of-state business. If you travel into another state to sell your products, you have created nexus in that state and will need to collect sales tax. For example, if you travel to another state for a speaking engagement or convention you may need to pay sales tax on your sales while in that state. State laws on transient sales vary by state, so check with each states' sales tax department prior to selling on location in that state. Here is a website to help: www.taxadmin.org/fta/link/

True Story: I was invited to be a speaker at a convention in Virginia (my home state is Ohio) and I sold books and CDs at my booth. Virginia did not ask me to apply for a vendor's license since I was only temporarily in the state, but I did have to pay sales tax on my total sales for the three days I was there. Fortunately, the convention hosts were very good about giving every vendor information and forms on Virginia's sales tax requirements. After the convention, I totaled my sales, filled in Virginia's sales tax forms and mailed a check to the state.

On-line Sales and Sales Tax

The opportunity to sell products on-line has opened the doors for thousands of authors and small business owners, but it has also created a lot of confusion regarding sales tax. On-line sales tax rules are emerging and you should expect to see changes in the years to come. For now, authors who sell on-line follow the same nexus rules for all small business: you do not collect sales tax if the customer is out-of-state (or you do not have a physical presence in that sate), but you must collect sales tax from customers in your state (or where you have a physical presence). The fact that your website can be read by people in all states, does not create nexus, or a physical presence, in those states.

In a Nutshell

A checklist of duties for dealing with sales tax includes:
- Learn about your state and local sales tax laws. Start with an internet search on your state and "sales tax."
- Know when customers may not have to pay sales tax. The tax exemption regulations vary by state.
- Set aside sales tax collected; do not spend it on your business expenses.
- Keep good records of all sales. Consider using QuickBooks or other accounting software.

- Make regular tax payments whether it is semi-annually, quarterly or monthly.
- Meet with a CPA to get help in tax planning and sales tax calculation.

CHAPTER 13

INCOME TAX FOR AUTHORS

In the chapter on business structure, I said that most authors run their writing businesses as sole proprietorships. This chapter will cover some tax aspects of a sole proprietorship with special emphasis on authors. As a sole proprietor, your business taxes are filed with your personal income tax return on IRS Form 1040. Partnerships and corporations file tax returns that are separate from their individual owners.

I focus on sole proprietorships because that structure applies to most authors.

Tax Form for Sole Proprietors: Schedule C

I know that most authors do not like dealing with numbers and especially taxes, but it is a good idea to become familiar with some important tax forms. Sole proprietors use the Form 1040 Schedule C Profit or Loss from Business to report their income and expenses. I recommend you look at the categories of expenses and then use them

SCHEDULE C
(Form 1040)

Department of the Treasury
Internal Revenue Service (99)

Profit or Loss From Business
(Sole Proprietorship)

▶ Partnerships, joint ventures, etc., generally must file Form 1065 or 1065-B.

▶ Attach to Form 1040, 1040NR, or 1041.   ▶ See Instructions for Schedule C (Form 1040).

OMB No. 1545-0074

20**10**

Attachment
Sequence No. **09**

Name of proprietor

Social security number (SSN)

A   Principal business or profession, including product or service (see instructions)

B Enter code from pages C-9, 10, & 11

▶

C   Business name. If no separate business name, leave blank.

D Employer ID number (EIN), if any

E   Business address (including suite or room no.) ▶

City, town or post office, state, and ZIP code

F   Accounting method: **(1)** ☐ Cash   **(2)** ☐ Accrual   **(3)** ☐ Other (specify) ▶

G   Did you "materially participate" in the operation of this business during 2010? If "No," see instructions for limit on losses   ☐ **Yes** ☐ **No**

H   If you started or acquired this business during 2010, check here   .   .   .   .   .   .   ▶ ☐

Part I   Income

1 Gross receipts or sales. **Caution.** See instructions and check the box if:		
• This income was reported to you on Form W-2 and the "Statutory employee" box on that form was checked, or	⎫	
• You are a member of a qualified joint venture reporting only rental real estate income not subject to self-employment tax. Also see instructions for limit on losses.	⎬ ▶ ☐	**1**
2 Returns and allowances		**2**
3 Subtract line 2 from line 1		**3**
4 Cost of goods sold (from line 42 on page 2)		**4**
5 **Gross profit.** Subtract line 4 from line 3		**5**
6 Other income, including federal and state gasoline or fuel tax credit or refund (see instructions)		**6**
7 **Gross income.** Add lines 5 and 6 . . . . ▶		**7**

when recording your business expenses to make tax preparation easier. Later in this chapter, I list many common business expenses that can be deducted on your income tax return.

Name and Number

The first few lines of the Schedule C are pretty straight forward with name, address and so on. A sole proprietor may use their Social Security Number or apply to receive an Employer Identification Number (EIN) from the Internal Revenue Service and record the EIN in Box D instead of their Social Security Number. To receive an EIN (at no charge), visit www.IRS.gov and search for "EIN." You can apply on-line, over the phone or by mail.

Many authors do not have a separate business name; you may simply use your personal name and leave line C blank. On the other hand, publishing companies have a unique name and need an EIN and record their business name on Line C.

Method of Accounting: Cash or Accrual

Line F Accounting Method can be a bit confusing. The cash basis of accounting is most common and it means that you report your income when the cash is received, regardless of when you did the work. This can happen if you submit a magazine article in November, but are not paid until February of the next year. In a cash-based accounting system you record the income in February.

The accrual system records income when it is earned, even if not yet paid. This would occur if you ship out a box of books and then wait to be paid. Usually, business owners that buy and sell inventory use the accrual system.

Recently the IRS has ruled that a small business may use the cash based accounting system even though they buy and sell inventory. That makes bookkeeping simpler for most authors. Check with your CPA to determine which accounting system makes the most sense for your unique situation.

Part II Expenses. Enter expenses for business use of your home **only** on line 30.

8	Advertising	8		
9	Car and truck expenses (see instructions)	9		
10	Commissions and fees . .	10		
11	Contract labor (see instructions)	11		
12	Depletion	12		
13	Depreciation and section 179 expense deduction (not included in Part III) (see instructions) . .	13		
14	Employee benefit programs (other than on line 19) . .	14		
15	Insurance (other than health)	15		
16	Interest:			
a	Mortgage (paid to banks, etc.)	16a		
b	Other	16b		
17	Legal and professional services	17		
18	Office expense	18		
19	Pension and profit-sharing plans	19		
20	Rent or lease (see instructions):			
a	Vehicles, machinery, and equipment	20a		
b	Other business property . .	20b		
21	Repairs and maintenance . .	21		
22	Supplies (not included in Part III)	22		
23	Taxes and licenses . . .	23		
24	Travel, meals, and entertainment:			
a	Travel	24a		
b	Deductible meals and entertainment (see instructions) .	24b		
25	Utilities	25		
26	Wages (less employment credits) .	26		
27	Other expenses (from line 48 on page 2)	27		
28	**Total expenses** before expenses for business use of home. Add lines 8 through 27 . . ▲	28		
29	Tentative profit or (loss). Subtract line 28 from line 7	29		
30	Expenses for business use of your home. Attach **Form 8829**	30		
31	**Net profit or (loss).** Subtract line 30 from line 29.			

Income

Part I of the Schedule C is where an author or publisher reports his or her business income returns and cost of goods sold. I discuss how to calculate cost of goods sold in Chapter Eleven on Inventory.

Expenses

The best way to reduce your tax burden is to take every deduction you are allowed. Business expenses that are income tax deductions are listed in Part II of the Schedule C.

Some of the common expenses for authors and publishers include:

- Advertising and promotional costs including your website, ads, bookmarks and business cards that serve as advertisements.

- Commission and fees. If you have an agent that takes a commission based on your royalties, record it here. Some authors prefer to put their Paypal or shopping cart fees from book sales in this category. The IRS allows merchant fees to be included in cost of goods sold, but some authors prefer the fees to be more visible so they know what they are spending on merchant fees. This helps them shop for a better plan.

- Car expenses. Use a mileage log or a calendar. The IRS requires the records be kept contemporaneously, meaning you should not rely on your memory. Estimates are not allowed; there must be actual mileage records. The IRS sets the per mile rate and adjusts it annually. For example in 2010 the mileage rate for business miles was $.50/mile. In 2011 it will be $.51 per mile.

- Contract labor for your editor, graphic designer, or anyone you hire as an independent contractor.

- Depreciation applies to purchases of computers, furniture or equipment that will last longer than a year. Depreciation is an accounting term meaning that the value of the equipment is deducted on the tax return over several years. A Section 179 expense means that the full cost of the equipment is deducted in the year it was purchased. Your CPA can determine whether you should depreciate your equipment expense or deduct all of it as a Section 179 expense. Depreciation calculations can be complex. Give your CPA information on your purchase including the cost and the date of purchase and he or she will calculate the correct deduction to use on the tax return.

- Insurance on your inventory or professional liability insurance on your business.

- Legal and professional services to lawyers and accountants. Other professionals are listed under contract labor.

- Office expense including postage, paper, ink, envelopes, etc.

- Taxes and licenses including sales tax paid to your state from book sales and business or vendor's licenses.

- Travel, meals and entertainment for business including writer's workshops and conferences. Deduct the mileage or car rental, lodging and one-half of the meals spent while on a business trip. If you take your spouse or family, only the portion for you, the business owner, is deductible.

- Utilities such as telephone, cell phone and internet service charges. The first phone line into a home is considered a personal expense and not deductible as a business expense. See my caution below about mixing personal and business use of telephones and the internet. Only the business portion is a tax deduction.

- Other Expenses. Some common business expenses for authors to include in this category include:
  - Books, magazines, and subscriptions. Any publication

that helps your writing and publishing business or is used in researching your book is deductible. The cost of this book is a tax deduction.

- Professional organization dues.
- Professional development to make you a better writer including classes, conferences and writers workshops.
- Fees to purchase an ISBN, a Library of Congress Number (LCCN) and bar codes, for your self-published book.

Take all the deductions you are entitled to but watch out for the following:

- **Printing**. The cost to print your book is part of your cost of goods sold, which is included in Part I Income on Schedule C. I discussed cost of goods sold in Chapter Eleven on Inventory. Do not put the cost to print your books under supplies or elsewhere in Part II Expenses.

- **Merchant fees** such as Paypal or website shopping cart fees. These fees can be a part of the cost of good sold but some authors prefer to list them under expenses. Frequently an author will only record the amount they are paid *after* the fees are deducted (the net sales after fees) for simplicity. In this case, merchant fees are not listed as cost of goods sold or as a separate business expense.

    Example: Your ebook may sell for $10.00 online, but after Paypal takes its processing fees, you receive only $9.50. You could record $10 of income and $.50 of merchant fees (as part of cost of goods sold or as an expense) or just record $9.50 income and no merchant fee expenses.

Either method will result in the same bottom line for tax purposes. The advantage of recording merchant fees is that you have visibility into the total expenses. The disadvantage is that it involves more record keeping.

- **Mixed use** (business and personal use) for internet fees, computer, cell phone, etc. You may only deduct the business portion of these shared expenses. The IRS does not expect a detailed time log, but has accepted a one month log as representative for the entire tax year. You could also use any reasonable allocation to separate personal and business use.

- **Business use of the home** is a business deduction, but only if the office portion of your home is used *regularly and exclusively* for business. An office cannot be used for writing and used by the kids for homework and be eligible for the deduction. Many authors may regularly use their office, but find the exclusive requirement to be difficult to meet and therefore do not take the business use of the home deduction.

  True Story: I have worked from my home office for ten years, but have never taken the business use of the home deduction because my daughters and husband also use my office. On the other hand, my neighbor, Ed, is a salesman with an office devoted solely to his work. His family uses a separate laptop in the family room for homework and personal e-mail. Ed is entitled to a business use of the home deduction, while I am not.

- **Personal Travel.** Avoid using a personal trip with the hope to write a book about it as a business deduction. It has been tried before and failed in tax court. Linda Lewis, an attorney has written an article titled "Authors and the Internal Revenue Code" . Ms. Lewis shares some vain attempts by authors to claim rather outrageous tax deductions. She also shares why and how some trips are legitimate business deductions. You'll find the article at Eclectics.com under Writing Articles.

Unique Deductions for Authors

The IRS tax code does have some special provisions just for authors. It is very common for an author to incur expenses in researching and writing a book. He or she may need to travel or buy reference books. In the past, these expenses could not be deducted until the book sold, and then in proportion to the book sales, meaning a little at a time, over several years. In accounting jargon, we call that "amortizing an expense." For authors, this amortization requirement was unreasonable. How many years would a book sell, if it sold any? Authors had no idea of how to amortize their research expenses.

In 1986, sanity prevailed and now authors can deduct their research fees as business deductions in the year they are incurred. Cyn Mason (www.forwriters.com/taxes.html) has written an excellent article on this issue. She states, "if you are an ongoing sole proprietorship incurring ordinary and necessary expenses relating to doing business during your tax year, you may simply write off your expenses in the year incurred exactly like any other small business."[3]

Be Aware of Self-Employment Tax

Most authors are aware that if they have a successful writing business, they will owe federal, state and perhaps local income taxes. What some authors do not know about is what I call the hidden tax on the IRS Form 1040: the self-employment tax.

If a writer has net income (profit) over $400 a year, he will owe self-employment tax *in addition* to federal income tax. Self-employment tax is the same as Social Security and Medicare for self-employed people and sole proprietorships. Self employment tax is calculated using Form 1040 Schedule SE and is approximately 15% of your net income. The $400 threshold has not been adjusted in decades. Many authors find that they may owe more self-

3 www.forwriters.com/taxes.html, "Taxes for Writers" by Cyn Mason, accessed 8/13/2009

Section A—Short Schedule SE. Caution. Read above to see if you can use Short Schedule SE.

1a Net farm profit or (loss) from Schedule F, line 36, and farm partnerships, Schedule K-1 (Form 1065), box 14, code A	**1a**	
b If you received social security retirement or disability benefits, enter the amount of Conservation Reserve Program payments included on Schedule F, line 6b, or listed on Schedule K-1 (Form 1065), box 20, code Y	**1b**	( )
2 Net profit or (loss) from Schedule C, line 31; Schedule C-EZ, line 3; Schedule K-1 (Form 1065), box 14, code A (other than farming); and Schedule K-1 (Form 1065-B), box 9, code J1. Ministers and members of religious orders, see page SE-1 for types of income to report on this line. See page SE-3 for other income to report	**2**	2000
3 Combine lines 1a, 1b, and 2. Subtract from that total the amount on Form 1040, line 29, or Form 1040NR, line 29, and enter the result (see page SE-3)	**3**	2000
4 Multiply line 3 by 92.35% (.9235). If less than $400, you do not owe self-employment tax; **do not** file this schedule unless you have an amount on line 1b ▲	**4**	1847
Note. If line 4 is less than $400 due to Conservation Reserve Program payments on line 1b, see page SE-3.		
5 **Self-employment tax.** If the amount on line 4 is: • $106,800 or less, multiply line 4 by 15.3% (.153). Enter the result here and on **Form 1040, line 56,** or **Form 1040NR, line 54** • More than $106,800, multiply line 4 by 2.9% (.029). Then, add $13,243.20 to the result. Enter the total here and on **Form 1040, line 56,** or **Form 1040NR, line 54**	**5**	283
6 **Deduction for one-half of self-employment tax.** Multiply line 5 by 50% (.50). Enter the result here and on **Form 1040, line 27,** or **Form 1040NR, line 27**	**6**	

employment tax than they owe in federal income tax (depending on their income tax bracket).

The self-employment tax is buried on the Form 1040 in the middle of the back page on Line 56. It is not in bold print like the federal income tax—that is why I call it the "hidden" tax. Also, many new authors are unaware that they owe self-employment tax until they prepare their tax returns and are surprised by a rather large number on Line 56 (the Self employment tax).

> True Story: Judy was pleased to make $2,000 in freelance writing one year and didn't think it would affect her tax situation very much. She knew she needed to report the $2,000 as income, but hoped she would not owe the IRS money because she had always received a tax refund before. Her CPA prepared a Schedule C Profit or Loss from Business and attached it to her individual Form 1040. What Judy did not expect was to be paying self-employment tax in addition to her income tax. Her self-employment tax was approximately $283. Page 104 shows what Judy's Schedule SE might look like.

Tax and financial adviser, June Walker, runs a great website for self-employed people including artists and writers at http://junewalkeronline.blogspot.com. June uses her blog to answer questions from what she calls "Indies" (short for independent workers), several of whom are authors.

Are Royalties Taxable?

A fortunate author writes a blockbuster book and collects royalty checks for years to come. Is that income taxable, even after many years? According to the IRS, royalties are taxable income. Publication 525 Taxable and Nontaxable Income states *"Royalties from copyrights, patents, and oil, gas and mineral properties are taxable as ordinary income."*

The IRS has a form Schedule E (part of the Form 1040) called "Supplemental Income and Loss from rental real estate, royalties, partnerships, S corporations, estates, trusts, etc." The word "royalties" is in the title of Schedule E and an author might think that this is the form to use to report royalties, but that is not correct.

IRS Publication 525 explains that self-employed artists should report royalties on Schedule C Business Income or Loss:

> *You generally report royalties in Part I of Schedule E (Form 1040), Supplemental Income and Loss. However, if you hold an operating oil, gas, or mineral interest or are in business as a self-employed writer, inventor, artist, etc., report your income and expenses on Schedule C or Schedule C-EZ.*

The reason for using a Schedule C and not Schedule E is that writing is an active, not passive, activity (even if it was performed years ago). Earnings from active businesses are subject to self-employment tax. The royalties mentioned on Schedule E are royalties from gas and oil and are tied to a piece of physical property. They are considered passive income and not subject to self-employment tax.

Example: Peter wrote a best-selling book 10 years ago. He is now retired from writing, but he still receives royalty checks four times a year from his publisher. When Peter files his tax return he includes his royalty income on Schedule C Business Income and pays federal income tax and self-employment tax on the income. Sometimes it seems odd to him that he is considered as a business owner for tax purposes when he retired years ago, but that is how the tax code is written.

Tax Planning

In order to avoid a surprise like Judy had in the example above, you should meet with a CPA for advance tax planning. The best time to plan is before the tax year ends such as October or November. If you meet with a CPA to discuss your business for the first time in February, it is too late for him or her to help you plan for the inevitable taxes you will owe. Your CPA can help you:

- Estimate your tax liability and calculate estimated quarterly payments.
- Set aside enough money to pay your income, self-employment and sales tax.
- Track your cash flow, so you can know how to plan for large expenses such as purchasing more inventory.
- Help you determine how much money you can withdraw from your writing business for personal use and how much to leave in the business for future needs.
- Help you plan to grow your business or change your plans.
- Determine the best way to depreciate purchases of equipment.
- Reduce your taxes and prepare for the future by investing in the proper retirement plans.

Use your CPA as a resource. They can do a lot more than prepare tax returns. CPAs have vast experience in helping small businesses grow and seeing sole proprietors be successful. In the next chapter I explain how to work with your accountant and offer tips in finding a good business advisor.

In a Nutshell

Writers do not like dealing with taxes, but it is beneficial to become familiar with important tax forms and allowable tax deductions. The best way to reduce your tax burden is to take every deduction you are allowed and fortunately, the US tax code does have some special provisions just for authors. While, most authors know about federal income taxes, many may not know about self-employment tax. A CPA can assist you in tax planning and setting aside enough money to pay both federal income tax and self-employment taxes. The best time to do tax planning is before the tax year ends such as October or November.

CHAPTER 14

WORKING WITH AN ACCOUNTANT

Some writer-business owners might delay working with an accountant until they think they can afford it, but this can be harmful to a new business. Knowledge that is too little or too late can be very costly.

Recently, a friend of mine was audited by the Internal Revenue Service (IRS). She was an author and had prepared her own tax returns for three years. Unknowingly, she had made several mistakes that any CPA (Certified Public Accountant) would have caught. The audit was an unpleasant and expensive experience and I wish that she had used a professional to prepare her tax return three years earlier.

What Can a CPA Do For You?

Allot some of your first expenditures toward getting good business advice and asking a professional to prepare your tax return. In addition to tax preparation, a professional accountant or CPA can help your business in several ways.

- Assist you with accurate record keeping.
- Explain the benefits and disadvantages of forming a partnership or becoming a corporation.
- Help you take all the tax deductions to which you are entitled.
- Determine your eligibility for business use of the home deduction.
- Calculate proper depreciation of business equipment.
- Prepare payroll taxes and filing payroll reports.
- Calculate estimated taxes (payments made to the IRS and your state during the year).

No one is an expert at everything, so I encourage you to focus on what you do best—writing and publishing—and leave tax and accounting matters to those who are the experts. To keep accounting fees down, you can hire a bookkeeper at a lower rate than a CPA or do all the record keeping yourself and only meet with your accountant when needed.

How Much Do CPAs Charge?

Naturally CPA fees vary depending on location and their experience. A typical rate for a one-hour consultation with a CPA might cost you $100 to $300. Many CPAs will meet with a new business owner for 30 to 60 minutes for no charge.

Many authors use CPAs for tax preparation only. A recent survey by the National Society of Accountants[4] found that the tax preparation fees for the following business forms:

- Sole proprietorship (form Schedule C): $212
- Partnership return (Form 1065): $551
- S corporations: $665
- C corporations: $692

---

4 www.webcpa.com/news/-52744-1.html?st=RSS

These fees do not include the tax return for the individual which averaged $229 for a Form 1040 with itemized deductions and a state return. The survey found that tax preparation fees vary by region and size of the firm.

Get a clear understanding of what your future accounting fees might be. Many accountants charge a set monthly fee or will work on a project basis, such as setting up accounting software. You should be able to accurately budget what the accounting and tax preparation fees will cost your business. If your accountant is vague about fees, you may need to work with someone that can be specific about their fees so that you can plan for the expense.

Questions to Ask an Accountant

Interview a potential accountant and ask these questions:

- Tell me about your business clients? Any authors or publishers?
- Could you share two or three names as referrals?
- How much do you charge?
- How often am I billed?
- What is included in your services?
- What is *not* included?
- How often will we meet? Where?
- What do I need to bring to our meetings?
- Why is bookkeeping important?
- Explain the reports that I will receive from you.

In a Nutshell

I may sound a little self-serving since I am a CPA, but *please get help with taxes and accounting when you start a business.* Seek out an accountant that has the ability to teach you the financial side of your business. You should feel comfortable with him or her and be free to ask questions.

To find a helpful professional, ask other small business owners in your area for their accountant's contact information or contact your state CPA society. Find a listing at TaxSites.com and click on the Associations link.

CHAPTER 15

COMMON BUSINESS AND TAX MISTAKES MADE BY AUTHORS AND PUBLISHERS

"The only real mistake is the one from which we learn nothing"
—John Powell

Mistakes can happen in any undertaking, but fortunately we can learn from the mistakes of others. This list of mistakes made by authors and publishers is not exhaustive, but it will certainly help you avoid making too many mistakes of your own.

Failure to have a written contract with a publisher, graphic designer, editor, etc.

Identify the commitments of both parties and formalize the agreements in a written contract. Draft an agreement that is acceptable to all of the parties. Having a written document is the best protection you can ever give to your business.

Lack of know-how

Many small businesses fail because the owner lacks knowledge in some aspect of business. You may be good at writing, but you may need help in setting up an accounting system or marketing your book. Find some advisers or a mentor. These people can be your family or friends, as long as they are knowledgeable. Professionals such as a small business lawyer and an accountant are vital to have as advisers. You can also seek the help from the Service Corps of Retired Executives (www.SCORE.org), who provide volunteer business counselors.

Spending too much money

It is very easy and even fun to spend money on logos, websites, business cards, etc. Until you have income from the business, you should avoid spending too much money in advance. Obviously, some businesses require cash to start, but authors can easily start a business on a shoe string, especially in this day of on-line businesses. Let the business pay for itself.

Spending too little money

There are some things you should spend money on to launch a writing business. Essential expenses include an editor and graphic designer for your book and an accountant for business advice. You may also need to spend some money on launching a website, although prices in that area have come down significantly in the past few years. Many people try to save money with cover art or layout and it shows. Budget and save until you have the money to launch your book correctly and professionally.

Working without a budget

You cannot control spending if you do not know where you spent your money. Tell your money where to go before it goes there by having a budget. Failure to plan is planning to fail.

Failure to reconcile bank accounts

You should reconcile bank accounts monthly to uncover mistakes in data entry by you or by the bank. Reconciling will also tell you where you spent your cash. Additionally, you need to know what checks are still outstanding so you do not spend money that may not be in the account.

Not having a filing system

A place for everything and everything in its place. Keep files for receipts, invoices, tax returns, government correspondence, contracts and bank statements.

Forgetting to backup your data

Your writing efforts are too valuable to lose, and so are your business records, so back up your data regularly. I have my computer system set up to do automatic backups to an external hard drive. It is a great feeling knowing that everything is saved twice.

Doing your own tax return

You are in business and should get professional assistance with your tax return. Focus on what you do best, writing and selling your book, and let the tax professionals do what they do best—tax returns.

Taking incorrect tax deductions

An incorrect tax deduction can mean you pay too much in taxes, or even worse, face an audit by the IRS. Learn what deductions are allowed. Your accountant can help you take every deduction you are entitled to take.

Failure to count inventory at least annually

It is very important that you count your inventory at the end of the year so that your cost of goods sold calculation is correct. You may be paying too much in taxes if you miscalculate cost of goods sold.

Poor record keeping

Studies show that business success follows good record keeping. Without good records, you will not know if you are making a profit or loss, nor will you know what sells well.

Failure to follow up on payments due to you

Keep a record of who still owes you money (called accounts receivable) and send reminders every 30 days. If a business (or individual) is past due more than 60 days, do not send them more products or continue doing business with them until they have paid off their current balance.

Worker misclassification

Treating a worker as an independent contractor when he or she should be classified as an employee is a serious mistake with tax consequences. The IRS takes worker misclassification very seriously. They have implemented a system where a worker can file a complaint against an employer. If the employer misclassified the worker without reasonable cause, they will be held liable for employer taxes on that worker. Read more at the IRS website, www.IRS.gov, and type 'worker misclassification' in the search box.

Failure to take a reasonable salary from an S or C corporation.

Authors or publishers that have structured their businesses as S or C corporations must take a reasonable salary. The salary is subject to income tax and employer taxes (Social Security and Medicare). There may seem to be advantages to taking a low salary and avoid self-employment tax, but the IRS expects an owner to pay himself a reasonable salary according to the industry standards and the amount of work put into the business. This issue of unreasonably small salaries has become a red flag to the IRS and a subject of many audits.

Misusing QuickBooks

QuickBooks is a great software program if used correctly. The old adage, "garbage in, garbage out" applies to QuickBooks. Make sure you are properly trained in its use. Tutorials, on-line assistance and books such as *QuickBooks For Dummies* can be very helpful. You can also hire someone to set up the software for your particular needs. Knowledgeable QuickBooks experts in your area can be found at Quickbooks.intuit.com by clicking on the Learning and Training link.

Mixing income and expenses in the same QuickBooks account

Avoid mixing income and expenses in the same QuickBooks account, because you will not have an accurate picture of your income, nor you expenses. For example, say you attend a convention and sell some of your books, but also incur travel expenses. If you mix these transactions into the same account called "Conventions," you will not have accurate data on the income made or the expenses incurred. Your accountant will spend needless hours untangling your transactions to prepare your tax return.

Co-mingling funds.

Mixing business and personal expenses in the same checking account or Paypal account can lead to a lot of confusion. The IRS may consider your personal deposits as business income in an audit if you cannot prove otherwise. Keep your business and personal expenses in separate checking accounts.

Depending on your memory instead of written records

Plutarch said, "Forgetfulness transforms every occurrence into a non-occurrence." If you rely on your memory instead of records or receipts, you are bound to forget some important tax deductions, or worse yet, a customer order. The IRS requires records, especially for mileage to be kept contemporaneously, meaning at the time the expense was incurred and not months later.

Neglecting to record mileage

You will be walking away from a tax deduction if you do not keep mileage records. Some business owners keep a mileage log in their cars while others keep track of business trips in a calendar. I make use of Google maps and use the mileage amounts for trips I make.

Failure to set aside money to pay income tax, self-employment tax or sales tax

Realize that not all the profit you make is yours to spend. The tax man wants his due. Tax planning with a CPA will keep you out of hot water with the government and let you sleep better at night.

CHAPTER 16

EXPERT ADVICE

The following authors and publishers share their experience of running a business. They were asked questions about their business structure, use of professional accountants, business mistakes they made, and what advice they had to offer. I think you will find their experiences very valuable.

Cathy Diez-Luckie, www.figuresinmotion.com, *Figures In Motion*

Tell me about your writing business and how you got started.
One book out in 2009, two books in 2010, two for 2011. Working on business since 2007. Started when I wanted to add interest to my children's study of history.

What is your business structure?
Sole Proprietorship

Do you use an accountant in your business?
Yes, but for tax preparation only. I now realize that I need a bookkeeper to help me make sure everything is accounted for.

With what task has your accountant been most helpful?
Giving me guidance on how to record transactions for my business.

What accounting issues are the most confusing to you?
Taxes, business structure, bookkeeping

What is one business mistake you made when starting your writing career?
Thinking that I would have time to work on my business whenever I wanted.

What business advice do you have for new authors?
To keep God, husband, and family always at the top of your priorities and work when God has given you the time to work. Don't get frustrated when you cannot devote the time you think you should have to your business. Unless the Lord builds the house (the business), its builders (you) will labor in vain. (A modification of Psalm 127:1)

If you could spend one hour with a CPA for free, what would you ask?
I would ask a CPA to help me set up my books and check whether I am entering things properly.

Mary Hood, www.archersforthelord.org, *The Relaxed Homeschooler*

Tell me about your writing business and briefly how you got started.
Five books plus CDs and booklets. Writing since about 1990. Got started after my Ph.D. was finished and I wanted to start sharing with other homeschooling families.

What is your business structure?
Nonprofit

Do you use an accountant in your business?
Yes, but for tax preparation only.

With what task has your accountant been most helpful?
End of the year taxes and interfacing with IRS.

What accounting issues are the most confusing to you?
Inventory, independent contractors

What is one business mistake you made when starting your writing career?
I stayed as a DBA too long. *Note: Mary is referring to owning her business as a for-profit entity under a fictitious name, a "Doing Business As" or DBA name prior to become a 501c3 tax exempt nonprofit.*

What business advice do you have for new authors?
Don't worry too much about doing something wrong or getting into trouble...and ask plenty of questions, even if you think they are stupid.

If you could spend one hour with a CPA for free, what would you ask?
Should I get more computerized, especially with inventory?

Christine Field www.MomLifeNavigator.com, Attorney Homeschool Legal Advantage

Tell me about your writing business and briefly how you got started.

I have always written and I'm not sure I could ever NOT write. Studying the law made me a careful researcher and writer, but being from a long line of literate Irish people made me LOVE to write. God has provided me an intersection of faith, training and talent - working for Homeschool Legal Advantage.

What is your business structure?
Sole Proprietor

Do you use an accountant in your business?
Yes.

With what task has your accountant been the most helpful?
I am by nature a bit scatterbrained. He has helped me be more meticulous about keeping records and documenting finances.

What accounting issues are the most confusing to you?
Depreciation!

What is one business mistake you made when starting your writing career?
Not keeping good records.

What business advice do you have for new authors?
Keep good records.

If you could spend one hour with a CPA for free, what would you ask?
Walk me through what deductions are available to me as a person with a home office.

Hal & Melanie Young, www.raisingrealmen.com, *Raising Real Men: Surviving, Teaching and Appreciating Boys*

Tell me about your writing business and briefly how you got started.
We've been writing magazine and journal articles for about 10 years, but this is our first book.

What is your business structure?
S Corporation

Do you use an accountant in your business?
No. I do it all myself. I want a bookkeeper for Christmas!

What accounting issues are the most confusing to you?
Taxes, sales tax

What is one business mistake you made when starting your writing career?
We were blessed to have started an S-corp before and to have great business advice from others, so we didn't make any serious mistakes.

What business advice do you have for new authors?
Do your research, ask for advice, act like a businessman from the beginning. If you keep books and do things right from the beginning, it will be much easier.

If you could spend one hour with a CPA for free, what would you ask?
Please help me figure out how to manage sales tax in a bunch of states that are different every year. Please help me understand payroll issues better.

Lorrie Flem, www.TEACHmagazine.com, *Welcome Home Daddy* and *Beauty on a Budget*

Tell me about your writing business and briefly how you got started.
50+ books in 12 years. I wanted to subscribe to a magazine for homemakers and couldn't find one.

What is your business structure?
Sole Proprietorship

Do you use an accountant in your business?
Yes, for bookkeeping and tax preparation; she works full time for me.

With what task has your accountant been most helpful?
Financial details.

What accounting issues are the most confusing to you?
Taxes, business structure, bookkeeping, tax deductible expenses, employees

What is one business mistake you made when starting your writing career?
Not hiring a personal assistant sooner.

What business advice do you have for new authors?
Only write what you are passionate and knowledgeable about.

If you could spend one hour with a CPA for free, what would you ask?
Tax strategies to keep my costs down.

JoJo Tabares, www.ArtofEloquence.com, *Say What You Mean* series

Tell me about your writing business and briefly how you got started.

I've been writing since I was nine years old. A homeschool mom learned I had a degree in Speech Communication and asked me to teach a class in my home for her shy daughter. I couldn't find a fun, Christian-based speech book that took it slow for shy kids, so I wrote one. Before my book was back from the printer, my class was full and folks were waiting on my doorstep to buy it for use at home.

What is your business structure?
Sole Proprietorship

Do you use an accountant in your business?
My husband does it. He works in accounting.

With what task has your accountant been most helpful?
Tax return

What is one business mistake you made when starting your writing career?
Apparently giving too much away for free which devalues your information product. Not listening to the Lord fully when He told me to do something and doing much more than He asked.

W. Terry Whalin www.TerryWhalin.com Author and Publisher

Tell me about your writing business and briefly how you got started.
I've been a freelance writer and editor for over 25 years. I started in magazines and have written for more than 50 print publications. For the last ten years, the bulk of my writing has been in the book area. I've written more than 60 books for traditional publishers. I'm currently a book publisher for my main occupation at Intermedia Publishing Group. In addition, I have freelance income from my writing online and in print from magazine articles and books.

What is your business structure?

My business is structured as a sole proprietor. I had an LLC when I was a literary agent but I terminated my LLC when I became a book publisher.

Do you use an accountant in your business?

Yes I have an accountant for my taxes that lends credibility, accountability, and professional help to my business.

4. With what task has your accountant been most helpful?

Calling to my attention business items which, if tracked, are deductible.

What accounting issues are the most confusing to you?

No real issues

What is one business mistake you made when starting your writing career?

At first, I attempted to handle the business aspects on my own without professional help using programs like Turbo Tax and Quicken for business. While good programs, it is better to have a live CPA to help you.

What business advice do you have for new authors?

Realize the importance of consistent recordkeeping and it can provide a huge savings on your taxes. Freelancers are taxed at the self-employed rate or one of the highest rates. You can lower that amount you owe through good record keeping—your mileage to business meetings and other such things make a huge difference at the end of the year.

If you could spend one hour with a CPA for free, what would you ask?

I do not have any pending questions.

Terri Johnson, www.knowledgequestmaps.com, *Map Trek* series

Tell me about your writing business and briefly how you got started.
10+ books in nine years

What is your business structure?
C Corporation

Do you use an accountant in your business?
Yes, but for tax preparation only

With what task has your accountant been most helpful?
tax preparation

What accounting issues are the most confusing to you?
Taxes, bookkeeping, employees

What is one business mistake you made when starting your writing career?
Not incorporating sooner

What business advice do you have for new authors?
If traditional publishing doesn't pan out, then pursue self-publishing. We couldn't be more pleased with the process.

If you could spend one hour with a CPA for free, what would you ask?
How much should it cost to prepare or complete tax forms. How can you find someone to take over bookkeeping when you cannot employ them full time?

CHAPTER 17

RESOURCES FOR WRITERS

Author's Website: TaxesForWriters.com

Choice of Entity

The choice of business entity can be confusing; here are several resources to help you learn more.

The American Institute of CPAs (AICPA) has information on forming a corporation and many other business issues on their Financial Literacy website: *www.360financialliteracy.org/*

Start Your Own Business (by Entrepreneur Press) by Rieva Lesonsky

Small Business for Dummies by Eric Tyson and Jim Schell

Start Your Own Self-Publishing Business (Entrepreneur Press) by Rob Adams, Jennifer Dorsey and Terry Adams

Limited Liability Company

The Limited Liability Company Center (www. limitedliabilitycompanycenter.com/) run by David K. Staub, a business attorney has many helpful articles on the benefits and disadvantages of forming an LLC. You can also find information on your state's forms and fees.

Your Limited Liability Company: An Operating Manual by Anthony Mancuso

Form Your Own Limited Liability Company by Anthony Mancuso

Limited Liability Companies For Dummies by Jennifer Reuting

Hobby Income
IRS article on hobby income "Is Your Hobby a For-Profit Endeavor?" www.irs.gov/irs/article/0,,id=186056,00.html

Charity and 501(c)(3) Tax Exemption

www.CarolToppCPA.com/services/nonprofit-consulting/ The author's website for nonprofit organizations

IRS website for charities and exempt organization www.irs. gov/charities/index.html

IRS report *501(c)(3) Organizations and Publishing Activities* www.irs.gov/pub/irs-tege/eotopice88.pdf

Software

Open Office. Free versions of word processing, spreadsheet and other applications: www.openoffice.org/

QuickBooks Products: quickbooks.intuit.com/

Peachtree Accounting Software: Peachtree.com

Online invoicing: FreshBooks.com

Online micro business acounting service: Outright.com

Online personal money management service: Mint.com

Free open source personal and small-business financial accounting software: GnuCash.org

EasyRoyaltiesUSA.com www.easyroyaltiesusa.com/

AnyBook Publishers Business Kit (www.ronwatters.com/ RonSoft5.htm)

Bookmaster: (www.ibsus.com/publishing-software/ bookmaster/) has several modules to handle all aspects of a publishing business including royalties, book productions, sales and returns.

Finding an Accountant

State CPA societies www.taxsites.com/cpa-societies.htm

QuickBooks ProAdvisor Referral program http://proadvisor. intuit.com/referral/

Income Taxes

Internal Revenue Service www.irs.gov

Article by Linda Lewis, an attorney, "Authors and the Internal Revenue Code" at www.eclectics.com/articles/taxes.html

Cyn Mason's article, "Taxes for Writers" at www.forwriters.com/taxes.html

June Walker's website for self-employed people including writers at junewalkeronline.blogspot.com.

Sales Tax

The QuickBooks Community http://community.intuit.com/quickbooks

Practical QuickBooks blog: http://qbblog.ccrsoftware.info/ Search for "Sales Tax"

State's tax laws at www.taxadmin.org/fta/link/.

Book Fulfillment

www.BookMasters.com

BCH Fulfillment & Distribution www.BookCH.com.

Writing and Publishing

Information in a Nutshell: Writing and Publishing by Felice Gerwitz
www.MediaAngels.com

Website for Authors:
www.InformationInANutshell.com

Radio for Authors

www.WritingandPublishingRadio.com

For more information about ordering this book or other books in the Information in a Nutshell Series, in bulk for wholesale or group discounts please email orders@mediaangels.com for information.